peace
AT THE
center

BY *David Dick*
DAVID DICK

First Edition, November, 1994

Second Printing, April, 1997

Cover design/illustration and book production
by Stacey Freibert Design

Back inset photo by Jim Loy

Illustrations by Jackie Larkins

Other books by David Dick

The View from Plum Lick
Follow the Storm
A Conversation with Peter P. Pence
The Quiet Kentuckians

ISBN: 0-9632886-2-8

Library of Congress Catalog Card Number
94-92164

for Lalie

CONTENTS

Part One - The Simple Things

Part Two - Remembrance

Part Three - The Yellow Brick Road

Part Four - Learning

Part Five - Liberty

Part Six - High Tide

Preface

"A foolish consistency is the hobgoblin
of little minds, adored by little statesmen
and philosophers and divines."

– Ralph Waldo Emerson –

After six years of doing just about everything my parents wanted me to do, 12 years of doing what my elementary and secondary teachers wanted me to do, six years of doing what college professors wanted me to do, four years of doing what the United States Navy wanted me to do, one year of doing what a retail chain store, an office equipment company, and a radio station wanted me to do, seven years of doing what WHAS Radio and Television wanted me to do, 19 years of doing what CBS News wanted me to do, and 10 years of doing what University of Kentucky administrators wanted me to do, I decided at age 65 it was about time for me to do exactly what *I* wanted to do.

I told the dean at the Institution of Higher Learning that I was going home to Plum Lick, and that this time it was for keeps. Douglas A. Boyd looked at me compassionately, his first impressions apparently long ago confirmed that I likely would not become durable, polished academic material. Nonetheless, with the dean's patient help, I had clawed my way to a tenured full professorship. I had done it without a Ph.D., and despite, or possibly because of, a Master's Degree in English Literature that was, at best, a strangely strung-out piece of quilting. I had tried to explain to Doug what I thought was a better way to live the Good Life, but he had always seemed more given to meticulously maintained European cars parked so thoughtless souls would not scratch them, while I drove un-ashamedly with cow manure on the bumpers of my pickup truck.

Dean Boyd and I had suffered each other rather kindly for the most part, and there were many times when we seemed to hit it off like two good old boys, despite our considerable dissimilarities. What he and other administrators understandably might have had trouble praising in a scholarly environment was my desire to write for everyday people who, I've always believed, want simple stories they seldom find anywhere else in the same kind of package. I would die a happy man just being *some* of the time a voice for Kentuckians, no matter where they might be in the world at any moment, as well as everybody in the other 49 states who secretly *wish* they were Kentuckians.

In my latest retirement, we will have one less car that used to maneuver with the driver as uptight as every other road hog out there on the interstate highway. Of course, we still have Ole Blue, the 15-year-old pickup truck, seldom seen off the farm these days. Ole Blue, a true "sport and mutation," has a gaping hole in the floorboard through which the driver is able to check the condition of the road at any given moment, while at the same time allowing its carbon monoxide all the freedom it feels it needs; the tailgate's rusted through so as to prevent easy access to the bed of the truck, where corn has been known to grow tall and tassel out. At last count, there are five older dogs and five puppies in residence on our farm (not including strangers and alien coyotes passing through) and five dog-whipped pussy cats including a few toms and one kitten. Depending on the season of the year, there're a small flock of sheep, a small herd of cattle, and enough space for humans to go out and pee on the ground when the urge arises, without anybody noticing.

I was maligned as being "disorganized" from the first to the last of my professorial years, but if being *organized* means methodically climbing the academic career ladder to a deanship, or, the Lord knows, a vice-chancellorship, or, goodness knows, a provost office somewhere between Carbondale and New York City, and running even the risk of missing such "disorganized" magic as a full moon setting before sunrise over Plum Lick, then all I can say is, they can have theirs and I'll hold on to mine. The truly organized administrator might calculate how to have both career and full moon, but I doubt I could pull it off.

I haven't gone off in a huff or a snit. Stretching all the way from early childhood to the hallowed halls of academe, folks have been tolerably good to me, and some have gone out of their way to be uncommonly helpful, although a few have allowed their mean-spiritedness to get the better of them. I won't try to name names because that might be libelous, and I have no desire to fight off lawsuits. You all know who you are, and you have to live with yourselves. I wish you the best of luck with whatever it is you make of the rest of your lives. I want each one of you to be at peace, and I'm sure you know by now, that's how I want to be.

Foreword

"God gives us love. Something to love
He lends us; but, when love is grown
To ripeness, that on which it throve
Falls off, and love is left alone."

– Alfred, Lord Tennyson –

Peace at the Center is the third of three books and follows *The View from Plum Lick* and *Follow The Storm*. It renews a search for inner contentment, individual control, a better truth, and, at least, an improved understanding of immortality.

The stories in *Peace at the Center* seek to build connections of community at a time when too many of the mass media—television, radio, newspapers, magazines, and all kinds of tabloid "journalism" —have systematically, some would say cynically, ignored the average person who lives a quiet life, who doesn't take hostages, who doesn't rob banks, and who seldom is recognized for simple and honest achievements based upon a value system considered at best outdated by "modern" life in the 1990s. The cacophony includes drugs, disrespect for established values, and mass media gone mad.

"Peace at the center" is a Quaker expression meaning serenity at the core of human, and, finally, spiritual life. There are many of us who believe it is not too late to turn around what appears to be a runaway cultural stagecoach headed for a great abyss where souls are in torment and the only sounds are discordant.

Just as there's a seed at the core of every apple symbolizing the physical world, at the heart of each seed deep within the elemental unit abides the opportunity for eternal life in the infinity of creation. The same is true for mankind. The outcome fundamentally depends on each individual's self-knowledge, self-worth, and self-starting energies.

After death has pared away the superficial surfaces of the physical self, leaving long, curling, and quickly browning rinds upon the earth—the fate of each member of mankind and all other creatures—it is then that the love within us passes over and may become eternally united with the Great Creator. In a whirlpool of universal energy, we join our truest selves with God, the ultimate love, and at last there's a probability of authentic peace at the center.

The problem, perhaps, is that the present generation, in the last quarter of the 20th century, is more concerned with comfort than with loveliness, more fascinated with unimpeded speed than with the slower swirl of snow on hillsides or the crunch of hooves in new fallen whiteness. Far too many, I think, prefer electronically generated graphics on television to finger tracings on frosted windowpanes.

In my quietest of moments, I think perhaps I'll spend some small part of the last ten or so of my three score and ten sitting in one of the several rocking chairs of this old house, reading good books, writing from time to time, more patiently awaiting the changing of the seasonal guards, the coming of another and, in time, final winter, when at last I will know more perfectly my personal peace at the center.

David Dick
Plum Lick, Kentucky
March 15, 1994

PART ONE

The Simple Things

Mr. Bo

"When the stars threw down their spears,
And water'd heaven with their tears,
Did he smile his work to see?
Did he who made the Lamb make thee?

– William Blake –

The snow had settled in before dawn on the third day following Christmas. It had begun after midnight as sleet, making the Plum Lick road slick and the walking slippery from the back door to the side gate leading toward the sheep barn. On the back porch of the old leaning house built about 1850, the temperature was zero in the first month of 1993 but the wind slicing paper-thin around the corners of the meat house made the air seem colder, much colder, cutting as it did against the face. It meant bundling up in the warmest clothes possible. Having shoes warmed by a night in the kitchen was a step in the right direction.

Bo was almost frozen to the ground. Ice crystals had formed on his legs tucked up beneath his slender body as if there might be an outside chance for warmth in that. There was nothing in his stomach, and his eyes were closed, but Bo had shone like a new silver dollar on a cold, clear winter morning. He was laid out as if for burying, or as if he had already been buried and hadn't been entirely covered over.

He could have been easily missed because he was 100 yards away from the flock of sheep that had gathered in the corner of the small pasture behind the corn cribs. In another hour, Bo's heart would have stopped beating. When he was spotted, the lamb had not yet been named Bo, short for Rambo. That came later in the warm kitchen.

"Let's name him, Rambo."

3

The shepherd's wife smiled and with the smile came the inevitable diminutive, always one of her special fondnesses, so that "Ruth" became "Roo," "Roger" became "Rog," and "Rambo" became "Bo."

"What happened to him?" she wanted to know.

"No mother in sight, at least none to claim him."

They had been through this many times. It had never turned out right. Orphan lambs were coming to seem as if they were impossibilities. Give them colostrum, first milk, taken from ewes that had lost their lambs; hold them warmly in loving arms to the side of the face; inject them with medications; send up prayers.

Yet, not until Bo did prayers seem finally answered. Not until Bo— stomach-fed with a tube, injected with a variety of animal medicines and human Vitamin E capsules—did the patient become too big for the cardboard box on the kitchen floor. Not until Bo did the family find itself holding extended although one-way conversations with a sheep.

"Hi, Bo!...Good morning, Bo...How's my baby?"

"Bet you're glad we don't live in California, aren't you Bo?"

"Bo, what do you think? Too much being made of the weather forecast? They're hollerin' more snow, you know."

After there was no doubt that the time had come to put him into the barn with the rest of the flock, the goodbyes were tenuous at first.

"Goodbye, Bo. Don't get caught in any slats."

"Don't let 'em smother you, Bo."

"Stand up for your rights, Bo."

"Butt with your best, Bo!"

An important commitment had been made. Any lamb falling to the cold hard ground, abandoned by its mother, and left to die on the spot deserved at least some extra consideration, a little peace at the center. Yes, his tail would be docked as all other lambs' tails were docked, because there's hardly anything more ugly or unsanitary than a sheep with a tail. Yes, he would have a plastic tag piercing his fine, fluffy outer right ear, but the "O" in "Bo" would have a smiley face with ears on the edges and a heart in the middle.

No, he would not be banded as most male lambs are, with the exception of those held back for breeding purposes, and Bo would *not* go to the slaughter house. For no imaginable reason would Bo walk the line at the slaughter house. He would not be pushed through the final door to be shot through his head, his throat slit, his body suspended on a hook, his blood spilling down the concrete sluice. Bo could live as long as he wanted. He could create life. He could become a symbol of hope. Bo would not be just another "dumb" sheep. He would even be allowed to graze in the yard. He would be the aristocratic, the irrepressible and irresistible Mr. Bo.

He had come at the end of the lambing season, and Bo had made up for all the little creatures that hadn't made it. He deigned to live in the barn, but whenever a human showed up, Bo came out to do the social graces. While all other lambs ran away from humans, Bo ran toward them, figuring every pant leg had a permanent milk faucet attached to it.

Bo's "maa" became distinctive, different from all the other "maas." Any "dumb" human could stand inside the barn door and pick out Bo's "maa." It had a "Here I am" ring to it, a "Be right there, so have that nipple up and running" urgency about it.

We took Bo with us to the Wool Fest in Falmouth last Fall, and although he didn't win any blue ribbons, he won hearts and brought out the smiles of many children, the way a tiny creature can save a winter for mankind. Just when frozen water buckets and birthing mishaps of every kind had made us doubt ourselves, along came Bo.

If something bad, really bad, ever happened to Bo there would be a void in our lives, a bruise that would hurt for a long time. But, in later life we've come to understand that we can never be sure about anything, and there's no guarantee that Bo would always brighten our days, no guarantee about ourselves, not about our bodies, not about our loves, not about the future. That's always been the gamble, the chance we take every day in human relations, especially with our closest loved ones.

Bo's message was always clear. Love now. Love well. There's no time like the present time. Try to look forward rather than backward, but remember, the most important thing of all is to take hold of each precious moment as if it were your last. It may be your last, but that doesn't mean it can't be your best. If we should go to the barn and if there were no Bo, all four legs scampering to find us, we could say to ourselves, he was here for a little time, and while he was, he brought us happiness we had not entirely known before.

Bo lived, and we loved him until the last day of winter in 1994.

"Dad," said the child, "Bo died."

"Where is he?"

"He's down there by the creek."

The family talked about what to do and decided that Bo would be buried on the knoll on the north side of the house. We picked a spot where there was a natural headstone. I began to dig. The soil was rich and there were only a few small rocks to be removed. I placed Bo in the grave and covered him over.

I could think of nothing to say.

No words came.

Later, in the quiet of the night, William Blake's poem lived, and so did Bo:

> *I a child, and thou a lamb,*
> *We are called by his name.*
> *Little Lamb, God bless thee!*

Cynthia

"Give me a look, give me a face,
That makes simplicity a grace."

— Ben Jonson —

The sun made a hazy appearance through the layered strands of clouds as daybreak began to spread beyond Bunker Hill. There, Bill and Lena still live on the ridge running southeast above the spot where a mobile home once stood, filled with the warmth of Ma Boyd: she'd lived most of the century from 1900 until last year when the Lord brought her home to bake hot buttered biscuits smothered in white-blossom honey for Timon, her husband and childhood sweetheart who'd gone before.

Even with its ice storms, the hard, cold, icy winter of 1993-1994 was mild compared to how it had been a century and a half before. Then, there was no electricity, no "modern" conveniences of any kind. There were only people, like Ma and Timon in the early 20th century, strong and resolute people, simple and determined, as great-grandmother Cynthia in mid-19th century, she the woman-child in her formal portrait with the severe face, the deceptively small hand draped down in front of her waist in the custom of the time, the black hair parted in the middle and the unrelenting, piercing eyes watching from over the mantlepiece in the front room of the house, which her great-grandson now calls "home."

Great-grandmother Cynthia bore eight children by two husbands and died at the age of 35, yet she hadn't died because she was weak-willed—she was as strong and as sharp-edged as a Shawnee flintstone. She passed on because the human body can only endure so much, when comes the moment that it fractures too. Cynthia's buried somewhere in a grave long since lost along with its headstone—perhaps she sleeps in the locust thicket up the hill from the log house built by her grandfather in the late 18th century at Plum, upstream from the meeting of Plum Lick and Boone creeks. Cynthia's second husband, John, may molder there with her, while they and their children—Little Ike, Jim, William, Mug, Elizabeth—and their children's children, are spread from Plum Lick like summer seed of nodding thistles, riding the rolling wind currents up and down the valley.

Well before Cynthia there had been Joshua, her grandfather, one of the early settlers of what Elder Samuel Rogers in a flight of unbridled enthusiasm later would call "the Canaan of the West," but what most others would come to know as "the Dark and Bloody Ground," the hunting province of the Shawnees. Josh and Polly Sr. had come down the Ohio River to the wilderness edge called Kentucky, leaving their homes in Pennsylvania and Delaware, and in 1799 they would purchase with British Crowns the land flanking both sides of Plum Lick Creek in eastern Bourbon County. To the pioneer couple had been born a daughter, who would live warm in memories as Polly Jr. She would marry William Hedges, who may have lived less than a mile away over the hill facing the west side of the homestead.

After Joshua and Polly Sr. had departed the valley on the wings of thistledown, Polly Jr. and William farmed on the home place, and to them had been born Cynthia in 1830, her simple essence still hovering 164 years later like a ghostly presence moaning with the coldest winds of winter through the Sycamores and the Water Maples along Plum Lick Creek. There's a distance of only about a quarter of a mile downstream to the piece of earth on which crumbles the original log house where Cynthia lived within the narrow walls of her brief existence.

She had less time than I, her great-grandson, to work out the nature of her peace at the center, because she was too busy living it to spend time thinking about it, much less writing about it. For Cynthia, peace at the center may have been nothing more than the silent work of her hands—the warmth of pot handles, the threading of needles, the patching of pants and often the legs inside, the churning of butter and the daily baking of bread, the washing of clothes, the feeling of the direct, insistent hardness of her husband when the moon was full and then the drifting off to sleep, the dreaming of dreams, the softness after the moon had finally drifted down the hills to the westward side of Plum Lick Creek.

The cutting of firewood was of central importance to great-grandmother Cynthia and great-grandfather John, for without a sufficient supply of firewood there could be hardly any life at all. Existence would be threatened in winter if late at night the warmth of the flagstone fireplace in the kitchen flickered and turned to cold ashes before sunrise. It would take more than one corncob daubed in fat drippings to resurrect a fire making it possible for a large family to line up in a file with backsides turned, nightgowns raised to capture the heat curling upward to that part of the body so resentful of biting cold.

The proper gathering of firewood was a year-round chore, not something to be thought of after the coolness of autumn had turned to the serious cold of winter about Thanksgiving time. Covering the distances through snow from the big house to the outhouse to the spring house to the meat house to the icehouse to the above-ground cellar to the barn became major trips not lightly undertaken. Each outpost had to have been considered carefully and tended well in advance of the harshest of winters: the cracks inside the outhouse covered with burlap sacks and a plentiful supply of crumpled paper laid by; the spring house cleared of accumulated mud, fallen rocks restored to their fitted places; the blocks of ice well layered with wheat straw; the foods preserved from the annual harvest, stored; the stalls bedded down and the corncribs filled with instant energy for the animals on frigid days and nights.

A hundred years later, some fundamentals had not changed, when Aldo Leopold wrote in *A Sand County Almanac:*

"There are two spiritual dangers in not owning a farm. One is the danger of supposing that breakfast comes from the grocery, and the other that heat comes from the furnace."

Peace at the center was not a seasonal diversion in mid-19th century; it was a daily, moment-by-moment way of life. It began with the relief Cynthia felt upon pushing another child from her body, holding the newborn to her breast, watching closely the drawing of the nourishment, the young mother at last looking upward into the dark, brooding eyes of her husband, John, silence attendant unto them.

The raucous noises coming a century and two world wars later would become enemies of this peace. The combustion engine alone would leave a lace of jet trails over Plum Lick from horizon to horizon, making the flight paths of geese seem less etched in purpose, the arrival of purple martins baffled and sometimes ruined by the wholesale application of insecticides. The whir of pickup trucks would replace the whinny of harnessed horses and mules. The screech of chain saws would be heard instead of the steady "chunk" of axes biting into wood, chips slicing away with measured, sweaty precision.

A century and more later, Pumpkin, the Australian shepherd, made no sound from her doghouse. Chip, the border collie, and Jeanne, the half-Australian shepherd/half-coon dog, were well past whimpering as they lay curled together on their bed of straw on the stone-cold concrete floor of the shop at the rear of the garage. At least *they* had escaped the steady march of "progress." Silence, except for the warmth of occasional barks, growls, and howls, continued to be one of their endearing traits, but they spoke with their eyes. Their silvery, ice-encrusted paws bore witness to their misery.

The weather forecast on Monday, January 3, 1994, included a winter storm warning of up to three or four inches of snow accumulation by Tuesday. The prediction was fulfilled with another inch or two in places like Plum Lick. Schools closed and stayed closed for the rest of the week. Children sat in front of television sets and looked for anything to break the "monotony." On January 5, snow began piling up in Kentucky in amounts of up to ten inches, the weather snapping power to over 30,000 people.

Schools re-opened the following week but closed again on Friday the 14th, after another snowfall and plummeting temperatures. By Saturday morning, January 15, 1994, the big thermometer on the back porch sank to zero, but the wind-chill factor was officially 36 degrees below zero.

Two days later, a winter storm warning continued for northern and eastern sections of the state with roads again put on ice— *sheets* of ice and freezing rain. On January 20, some interstate highways were re-opened, the front page headline in the following morning's newspaper a-hollerin': "Interstates crawling back to life." But the winter of 1993-1994 wasn't finished. On March 9, "Ice Storm II" came in with sleet, freezing rain, an inch of snow and, this time, ice four inches thick over already frozen ground. It left hundreds of thousands of people "powerless" in several southeastern states, one newspaper headlining it: "Powerless as in no hot coffee, lights or TV. Powerless as in the sky is falling."

Cynthia was lucky not to have had television and then lost it. Without it she was never revulsed by violence, sexual innuendoes in sit-coms grown blatantly crude, and the worst to be found in what CBS News would sanctimoniously call, "Reality Check." Cynthia didn't begin her day with programs such as "Breakfast for your Head" and she didn't require "morning" newspapers arriving at midday to tell her what had *not* happened in her community yesterday. What was happening in her neighborhood was, on the face of its individual self, simple and powerful with its own beauty.

There were her husband, John, her children gathered around her, the birds returning in spring, the quiet contentment deriving from the homestead established by her grandfather, Joshua. There was rich intimacy in the daily experience of feeling, touching, seeing, hearing, and breathing the fragrances of the land.

Cynthia's world was not perfect, far from it, but she may have understood its imperfection as a vital component of nature. She survived the cholera epidemic at mid-century, she set her body against every storm coming from any direction in the valley of Plum Lick and she lived to see the merciful end of the American Civil War. There were many imperfections: poor roads, few books, primitive schools, careless agriculture and inadequate medicine, which doubtless contributed to her premature death. Yet, although many lives were shortened and often tragedy struck harshly, Cynthia, her husband John, and their contemporaries acted from their individual resolves. After her passing, the responsibility for raising six small children rested with great-Grandfather.

The birthing of children had unquestionably stolen Cynthia's life, but who would dare say that the love within her was not passed along—that it does not live today in me?

Snowbound

"Blow, blow, thou winter wind,
Thou art not so unkind
As man's ingratitude."

– William Shakespeare –

*M*ost everybody on Plum Lick had been saying it for the past ten years: "We're going to have a *real* winter one of these times."

When Marvin Hedges came down the steep hill above Workman's Grocery in the heart of Plum to head over our way and help feed sheep, it didn't take a weather forecaster to tell him there was a sheet of ice to be respected. The county scraper had come through, leaving one good lane between the snowbanks, but the ice wasn't going anywhere for a while. About a foot of snow had fallen, and the temperature had taken a nose-dive. On the Bunker Hill side of Plum, Pete Hinkle said his thermometer registered 36 degrees below zero.

Billy Dale never missed a day feeding cattle with his tractor or his four-wheel drive pickup. Slipping and sliding up and down the hills from the hay pen to the cattle ricks took courage but especially it meant determination that no creature that could get up and walk was going to go hungry.

Three young calves disappeared. They could have become lost, or the coyotes may have had a feast. One calf showed up days after the storm, but the other two were goners, including the fine bull calf we'd thawed out in our bathtub before the storm hit.

"One thing about it, Billy, if the calves are dead there's nothing we can do to bring them back, and if they're alive there's no way we could carry them in, no place to put them even if we could."

Billy agreed.

The sheep fared very well. The mamas had enough wool on them to see them through worse than this, but not a whole lot worse. The lambs tucked in their behinds a notch, because their banded tails were dropping off, and it was a trifle airish up underneath there. All the sheep wanted was baled hay thrown down to them from the barn loft, and they were right interested in several bucketfuls of corn from the crib. Other than that, it was mamas nursing lambs as usual.

We have television down here, and sometimes (providing we haven't lost "power") we even turn it on, especially when there's a pretty good story like the winter of '94, which is what we guess they'll name this one. You would have thought the snowbirds were about to lose it. Maybe if they'd stay in Buffalo, where everybody "knows how to drive," or stay in Florida once they're down there, then we in Kentucky wouldn't have to be so concerned.

After the Governor of Kentucky had the good sense to close all interstate highways in the commonwealth, consider the fellow who said on television after they'd brought him in from his car on Interstate 75 up around Dry Ridge, warmed him up and fed him, and recommended that he stay there for his own safety as well as everybody else's: did we hear him right? We thought he said, "I feel like I'm in jail, and the Governor put me here."

Lord have mercy. If that had happened at Plum, Ray and Pete and Marvin and Billy and Johnny and Sweetpea would have given that fellow a blank stare which any poor soul could have read to mean: "Start walking. If you think you can drive, more power to you. We'll be here when you get back, if you get back, which you probably won't."

As for the Governor, it was reassuring to see him live on Kentucky Educational Television, which had the good judgment to provide the messages to the commercial stations, and to hear him asking people not to drive if they didn't absolutely have to. It sounded about right.

As for the complaint that Kentucky doesn't have once-every-ten-years snow-and-ice-moving equipment, that doesn't make too much sense. When the folks up north get tired of driving *through* Kentucky they can experiment with driving *around* it. We'll still be here, the way they were up there at Dry Ridge in Grant County, giving anybody who needs it a warm place to sleep and three square meals a day.

The winter of '94 put me to remembering the blizzard of '50, when I buried my mother's new Chevy in a snowbank on the road between Paris and Winchester. I walked to a farm house where a family and a few others had taken shelter. There was no television and for three bone-chilling days we ate a lot of green beans preserved in jars. There was an elderly woman in bed who should have been in a hospital. Snow had drifted along the inside walls of the house, and outside chickens froze where they fell. But there was nobody in that house who complained, and I don't remember anybody saying they felt like they were in jail.

The winter of '94 gave us a chance to stay home, and although we listened with some concern to the snapping sounds of the ice-laden boughs of the 80-year-old Water Maples surrounding the house, we watched the ice crystals on the windows lit by the break of day. Bundled up in blankets and sleep, we received with gratitude the help of neighbors and accepted the season for what it was intended to be: a better preparation for the coming of spring, when we hoped the travellers would return and feel better about it.

I had settled into my sleeping bag on the floor of my office that Thursday night at the University of Kentucky. I was there because I had found a window in the advancing frontal system and had hurried from Plum Lick to Lexington to be more sure of "being there," one of the fundamentals of a serious journalist, which I preach religiously to students. When I awoke Friday morning, I heard on radio that my nine o'clock class had been canceled. I went out to buy a morning newspaper, and I slid most of the way, going and coming.

"The ice age cometh," I mumbled to myself, professorially.

There was hardly anyone in sight. Trees were bending low with the weight of their icy mantles, the cold wind turning creaking murmurs into snapping sounds of surrender. A wandering Kentucky cardinal low on its luck, displaced from its mate, uttered mournfully, "What-cheeeer?"

My mate had called on the telephone and said, "We have no electricity, no water, no heat, no how."

As soon as possible, I headed home to Plum Lick: "Where I belong," I reminded myself.

The city streets had become lanes less traveled, and the interstate eastward was all right as long as speed and the distance between cars and trucks were minded cautiously.

I exited carefully at KY 11 and stopped at the Judy crossroads in Montgomery County, where I asked friends for advice at the J and M Food Mart.

"How's the Bunker Hill Road?"

"Solid ice."

Within about seven miles of home, the decision was to gamble. I wanted to "be there."

"Cut the ignition if you start to slide," came one of the several pieces of advice through the J and M door as it closed.

"Give us a call if you need help."

There was no traffic on the Bunker Hill Road for about three-and a-half twisting, turning, up-and-downhill miles, until the steep rise leading up to Bunker Hill Grocery. Near the top, several men were using a four-wheel drive truck to pull a car out of the ditch. Another car had gone off the road on the other side.

I stopped at the bottom of the hill and waited, no more than a mile and a half from home. Finally, the men decided to wave me on up to the top. The car started smoothly. It held speed up to the spot where the other cars had met their match on ice. Then it stopped and spun just enough to tell me I was going back down the hill.

For a few seconds, I managed to roll backwards in a fairly straight line. I tapped the brakes, quickly, lightly.

"Cut the ignition," I heard a voice echoing from J and M at the Judy Crossroads.

I cut the ignition.

What happened next was slow motion. I saw the drop-off on the driver's side of the road. "Is your seat belt fastened?" a calm voice asked from somewhere deep inside my mind. "Don't panic," another kind presence chimed. The car was now perpendicular to the road, the front wheels perched on the edge, one inch from the drop-off.

Four men came quickly down the hill. Three stood in front of the car and physically held it on the road away from its nose dive into the drop-off. The fourth man used a shovel to break ice, creating pivot points for the car to complete a 180-degree turn.

I'd been saved from a possible rollover and who knows what else, maybe *fire* and ice. The distance between life and death narrowed, and there were only seconds of time separating two worlds within the universality of God, but this was not *my* moment to cross over.

"Time to walk home," I said, reaching for my briefcase and a book on George Wallace I was reviewing for the *Lexington Herald-Leader.* I could hear the governor loud and clear:

"You know those pointy-headed professors can't park their bicycles straight...ask 'em to open up their briefcases and probably all you'll find inside is a peanut butter sandwich."

I not only couldn't have parked my bicycle straight, I couldn't even walk up the hill. One step forward, two steps back, a half-step forward, three steps sideways and back. The four men who by then were back at the top of the hill were watching the show. It wasn't pretty.

One of the men came down in his four-wheel drive, and as so often happens in a small community, he turned out to be a distant cousin.

"I'll take you home."

Even pointy-headed professors understand that kind of talk. Cousin Terry drove me to the top of Bunker Hill, then down the last mile on the Plum Lick Road to my gate, where he let me out so I could slide with whatever pride and dignity I had left in me the last quarter-mile to the house I call home.

It was a cold and dark home sweet home.

No electricity. No power to pump water. No juice to run the oil-fueled furnace. Refrigerator, dead. Freezer, dead. Kitchen stove, dead. Television, dead. Radio, dead. There was a telephone, but no reason to call anybody, although Cousin Marvin didn't have to be called. In zero-degree weather, he, driving his tractor with his wife, Reda, riding behind in an open trailer, brought over buckets of coal, containers of water, and a complete turkey dinner with all the trimmings.

From that Friday in February to the following Sunday night, the three of us, Lalie and I and our daughter Ravy, slept on the hearth of the house built in 1850, and we had a little taste of what it was like back then, causing us to appreciate the view from Plum Lick and certain basics that go with it a whole lot more. For us, the most important thing was, we were *alive*! Sixty-four hours later, when the Kentucky Rural Electric Cooperative lineman came that Sunday night and the power was restored, Lalie went out to deliver a "thank you" personally to the workers while the pointy-headed professor pulled the covers over his head and went to blessed sleep in the bed where he knew he belonged.

Sweet Owen

"He is the happiest, be he king or peasant,
who finds peace in his home."

– Goethe –

*T*here's something about the soil that pulls me back, it's dear to me, it pulls me," said Sara Betty as she headed northeast out of Owenton on Highway 22. She slowed the car as she approached the spot where once stood the store, with the words painted in red: "E.C. Ellis Gen'l Mdse." Sara Betty stopped. She turned off the engine and got out to stand close by the six-trunked Water Maple.

When she was a little girl she was Sara Elizabeth, the only child of Ernest and Maude. Sara Betty grew up in "Sweet Owen," a village taking that name from a grateful U.S. Congressman, John C. Breckinridge, whose narrow margin of victory in 1853 had been assured by the votes from Owen County. He had exclaimed (according to the way Sara Betty remembers it told to her): "God bless the vine-clad hills of sweet Owen." There's "Old Sweet Owen" and there's "Lower Sweet Owen," and for time out of mind there has been, most likely always will be, just plain "Sweet Owen." It was officially created on April 12, 1819, and named for Colonel Abraham Owen, killed in the Battle of Tippecanoe early on the morning of November 7, 1811.

Tears come to Sara Betty's eyes when she remembers her father and mother and how hard they worked in the store on Highway 22. "In 1929, the bottom fell out. Fine people didn't have money. He carried them for two or three years. People traded eggs for merchandise. Old Uncle Sam would come and say, 'Give me a pound of your best coffee, Uncle, the 60-cents kind, only the best, I want only the best.'"

Sara Betty remembered the men gathered around the hot stove, listening and awkward in the knowledge that the old-timer was barely able to scrape up enough to feed himself and old Aunt Susan too. Mr. Ellis, a proprietor who by practice as well as nature understood the innermost necessities of his customers, weighed out *two* pounds of 30-cent coffee, tied it up, and handed it across the counter to his friend. Old Uncle Sam put Mr. Ellis' "best" in the closing space between his arm and ribs, and he shuffled off with dignity in the growing pain of his steps. The men in the circling warmth of the store smiled respectfully and went back to their checkers, interrupted only as needed by such trifles as words.

Sara Betty loves to write about her native "Sweet Owen," and there are so many people, so many happenings she wants to include: how her mother and father finally had to give up the store in 1946; how lightning struck the old building in recent years and burned it to the ground; yet how the memories stay in her mind and will not be erased. There were the barrels of salt and crackers and sugar and lemonade, and the gray hearse pulled by horses that stopped in front of Mt. Hebron Baptist Church; there were the neighbors, Ladema, Odella, Eureba, and Rhetta Mae; there were dear old Mr. Joe and Beulah, Uncle Chippie, and Florinda, who washed for 14 families, washed and starched for them; there was Uncle Bip; and there were Lindsay and Eva, who were married for 75 years; there was "No Head Hollow" and there was the terrible thing that happened to a mother and her three children as they crossed Stevens Creek in a wagon when the water was running high—a log crashed into the slab bridge, the horse reared backwards, one of the wheels of the wagon dropped over the edge, the children spilled out, and two of the children drowned...and the mother was never the same after that. There was the little old man who kept bees and sold lard cans full of chunk honey; there were the sermons in Pleasant Ridge Baptist Church, where the sign in 1993 read: "Come in for a Faith Lift;"

there was Uncle Dan who ran the blacksmith shop; and there was Ernest who said, "A man doesn't have a right to leave the land worse than he found it."

Sara Betty remembered how on hot summer nights she and her father slept on blankets beneath the six-trunk Water Maple. One glorious evening she saw the aurora borealis, the northern lights, when the sky over "Sweet Owen" was awash in color.

At the end of a Sunday drive through "Sweet Owen," the lasting values of generations of people had been recalled; the green and graceful countryside had been recognized for its rich possibilities for those with the resolve to return to their roots, if only for a few precious moments.

It had done the soul good.

Home

"You can't go home again."

– Thomas Wolfe –

*I*t's my belief that you not only *can* go home again, but that you probably should. Now may not be the time, but most likely the best time will come. It will not be a perfect time, however, for as in Ecclesiastes: "To every thing there is a season...."

It's not unusual and it's probably natural for young people to try to get *away* from home—away from its bondage, its curfews, its perceived hypocracies, its narrow focus, its old habits, its conclusions rooted in the belief that no new dog should be taught an old trick. Wanting to get away from all of these "evils" is understandable and potentially healthy. It's an elemental case of wanting to try individual wings. That's what we were meant to do.

But after we've been shot down a few times, after we've swept in low over the green valleys, looking for better landing places, there'll come the moment when we will understand that it is time to go home again. Thomas Wolfe said you *can't* go home again, because he understood the feeling that comes when we go whistling down the lane toward the rose-covered cottage of our imaginations, only to find the paint cracked, the roof leaking, the porch fallen off, or worse yet, at the hallowed spot where the cottage used to be there's an interstate highway. Maybe the loved one who has been waiting for the prodigal son or daughter to return doesn't hear or understand what it is we're trying to say, and is puzzled by the tears on our faces.

Old relationships that once seemed so wonderful now play games with our good intentions. Differences can be very subtle, but no less real. For all these reasons, Thomas Wolfe said: "You can't..."

The reason lies in change, and the emerging truth is shaped by it.

Home has changed. We have changed. Those left behind have changed. Tennyson's "ringing grooves of change" create new patterns for the future, and if we accept the precept and let go of our yesterday selves, we not only recognize change but we accept its inevitability.

That's when we're ready to go home again, and it's good, because home is a pleasant and essential structure for love. It becomes a fundamental element within a community of homes filled with potential love, a prospect for universal peace at the center.

I left home in the bluegrass of Kentucky because I wanted to see the world. I wanted to test love against new standards in different situations. I wanted to go on deck to breathe Pacific air, to feel against my face the cold bluster of the Atlantic, to savor the Mediterranean, to stand in silence by the Sea of Galilee. Only after a quarter of a century, when I'd seen a good bit of the world from Tokyo to Beirut, from Montreal to Montevideo, was I ready to go home again.

The Homecoming

"She'll be comin' 'round the mountain when she comes,
She'll be comin' 'round the mountain when she comes,
She'll be comin' 'round the mountain,
She'll be comin' 'round the mountain,
She'll be comin' 'round the mountain when she comes."

– Traditional –

an you live on your hogs, your chickens and your garden?" Of course he could, and he did, with the help of his able sons. A determined man with a loving wife and loyal sons and daughters by his side has been known to be unbent by the strongest of winds.

The words appearing in "The Thunder Baby" story in my first book, *The View from Plum Lick*, had begun to haunt me, so I picked up the phone and called June, one of the granddaughters of John Jefferson Prather—one of the patriarchs of Plum Lick, who lived in "our" house from 1917 to 1941. He passed away at the age of 84.

"June, why don't you and the Prathers hold your next reunion here at the old home place?"

"When?"

"Anytime."

"How about September?"

"That's fine. Will you be calling Johnny?"

Clarence, Will, Ernest, Charlie, Tom, Reed, Russell, and Joe — the Prather boys who tilled the soil on Plum Lick and sowed the seeds for new generations of farmers and city dwellers.

I had also written about June's brother, Johnny Prather, in *The View from Plum Lick*. We'd gone to the 7th grade together in the old Little Rock school more than 50 years ago. And that's how it came to pass that on a Saturday in September of 1992, the Prathers started arriving at the house where John Jefferson Prather had lived out his years. In all, 91 descendants from Kentucky, Tennessee, Ohio, and North Carolina made the pilgrimage to the spot where three-quarters of a century before, John the patriarch and his eight sons—Clarence, Will, Ernest, Charlie, Tom, Reed, Russell, and Joe—stood in a row to have their formal picture taken in front of the house facing Plum Lick Creek.

John Jefferson Prather, 6 feet 4 inches tall, faced to the south, as a captain on the prow of a sailing vessel, while the sons, out of respect for their father (or fear), looked to the west toward the curves of the hills, where the sun and the moon still do their settings.

The matriarch, Kate Reed, and the three of their four daughters—Essie, Catherine, and Mary (Alma died when she was but 21)—deferred to the men, but in time the girls began their own families, created their own traditions, and secured their rightful places on earth and in immortality. Attempts to standardize political correctness and gender equality had not yet been visited upon the land, and families such as the Prathers lived naturally as a segment of society, beholden unto itself and not the contrivances, which in time would follow at the Institutions of Higher Learning and the corporations of mass media. The Prathers were a people who knew who they were, and they knew they didn't have to explain the realities of it to anyone outside the family unless they chose to do so. If at a later time it would be dismissed as bull-headed, insensitive rural clannishness, then so be it. The picture of the three surviving daughters, the eight sons, Kate, the matriarch, and John, the patriarch, would speak for itself.

In the picture in front of the house, "Pap"—"When he spoke, you listened"—and his "boys" placed their hats upon the ground by the toes of their shoes, a sign of disarmament and attending peace. Watch fobs hanging from belts were symbols of pre-depression better times. Later, when the bankers threatened foreclosure, the stern, rigid, sober John Jefferson Prather "...cried unashamedly before them not to take his land away from him."

He held on stubbornly and rode out the storm, and when he died a half-century ago, family and friends came from far and wide to say good-bye to the patriarch, who loved to read his Bible every day, expected everybody to be out of bed early, and quit work by five in the afternoon.

"When he came to this [part of the] country from Magoffin County in the Eastern Kentucky mountains, all he had was a shirt, two pairs of pants, and the horse he rode in on," grinned grandson Johnny.

"No money?"

"No money. He believed in hard work. He ran the farm until he died."

"Over there," said granddaughter Betty Jo, "was where the steps used to go upstairs."

"About over there," said grandson Charles (or was it grandson Billy?), "was where the pine tree stood," where the "boys" had their picture taken, as they hung from the branch stobs, making grown men look like eight smiling monkeys. The pine tree has long since vanished, and the eight boys have all passed to their peaces, but the contour of the land continues on the slopes to the north, where at night the Big Dipper hangs, waiting for angels to pause for a drink.

All afternoon beneath the giant Water Maples, where food was spread on tables, plenty of fried chicken and all the fixings, the descendants stood and sat and reminisced, the children playing with Chip, the new border collie puppy, until he was just about worn out from it, the new generation of daughters checking out the above-ground cellar and the "Big Spring" in the bottom land between the old house and the creek, the Reverend Charles Perry climbing up onto the above-ground cellar to take pictures of the 91 descendants for those who would come to this hallowed spot on God's earth in the year 2042.

As the Prather clan began departing in the year of '92, grandson Johnny placed one foot on the bottom plank of the fence in front of the house that has been home to so many, and he looked to the west and he said of the homecoming: "This was worth a million dollars."

In 1993, there were about 125 Prathers from at least five states, and in 1994, 111 homecomers had come "'round the mountain."

> We'll be, oh, so glad to see them when they come,
> We'll be, oh, so glad to see them when they come,
> We'll be, oh, so glad to see them,
> We'll be, oh, so glad to see them,
> We'll be, oh, so glad to see them when they come.

The eight sons and three daughters—Essie, Catherine, and Mary—of John and Kate Prather, the family who lived with love in their hearts for all the homecomings of the future.

RATS

"How now! a rat?"

— William Shakespeare —

*T*he rats in the attic and in-between the walls of our slowly sagging, ever-leaning, 1850 house sound like firemen rattling up ladders to put out five-alarm fires. Sometimes they remind us of point guards, lean and mean forwards, and towering centers thundering past full-court presses, slam-dunking with wild abandon. At other times the rat racket becomes so loud it wakes us up from deep sleeps and causes us to curse both the riders and the nights.

They are some right smart critters, sleeping by day, robbing banks by night. They rip and run like drunken sailors, and they have quickly discovered the combination to the dog food bin on the back porch. Restless about remembering numbers, they have left hard, black rat poop on the way out, their calling cards becoming ultimate insults.

"See you next time."

"What do you think we are? Stupid?"

"Share and share alike!"

"Why don't you get a little higher protein stuff next time?"

"Actually, the pellets are more convenient, so if it's all the same to you..."

The rats on Plum Lick have become so brazen it's a wonder they don't pull up chairs at sister Jane's white, close-kneed breakfast table. If sister Jane were alive she would have put a stop to this unholy mess sooner than we finally did. Sister Jane, like our mother before us, didn't suffer rats kindly, much less gladly. Those two ladies would have gone to the attic and beaten the enemy's brains out with baseball bats. I'm afraid that where they would have terrorized, we temporized, a sure sign of general weakness in the last decade of the

20th century. The net effect suited rat strategy to an R-A-T.

The present lady of the house could stand it no longer. The gentleman of the house was ambivalent and generally disinterested. He had more important things to do at the Institution of Higher Learning and heightened political correctness, where he repaired early each morning to deal with nobler motives and behaviors, while the lady stood with her aproned stomach pressed against the kitchen sink. She looked through the small back window, saw the latest calling cards, heard one last late night reveler staggering joyfully through the wooden passageway in the eave above the back porch, and Miss Scarlett said in her sweetest, lowest, most menacing tones from the deepest recesses of her soul: "I'm going to get you sons of bitches."

She climbed into the old station wagon with 180,000 miles on it and headed for town. She stormed into the hardware store, and she had "mission" written all over her softly smiling face. She made her purchases, turned on her heels, and returned home with traps, which she carefully positioned in the attic, on the edge of the canyon between the tired and chinked old walls, and in and around the dog food bin on the back porch. The strangers in the night either thought it was funny or considered it only briefly before dismissing it as mildly competitive but not very creative. The traps were obviously low-hurdle challenges to certified, card-carrying rats.

One rat miscued. S/he was, as they say at the Institution of Higher Learning "out of the loop," or "not on board when the train left the station." S/he sniffed the bait too closely, springing the trap, causing the lethal wire to come down like a guillotine blade, breaking but not severing the sable spine.

We heard the pop in the middle of the night.

"Got him!" cried Miss Scarlett.

Yet, by dawn's early light the rat pack undertakers had already conducted funeral services. They had come in the middle of the night like medics to the battlefield, and they had returned their own along the complicated maze of passageways to the attic inner sanctum, where the fallen was remembered with full honors. Out of respect and with no small degree of decorum, there were no calling cards left behind.

"Rats have mothers too," said the professor on his way to the university.

"I'll get the mothers too," said Scarlett.

She returned to town and shopped for the latest thing in rat poison, a product that dehydrates its victims, sending them on maddening missions in search of water to drink, which becomes the cocktail of death, the water triggering the lethal chemical formula.

All was quiet again on the Plum Lick front. Scarlett was appeased and serene once more. The battlefield was clear and clean. If a pin were dropped in the attic or between the walls of the old house, the sound would be heard and, perhaps, it would have signified a respite from the deathly silence that had become a reminder of simple creatures that also claimed this spot on earth as a place to BE.

They had lost, and our "victory" seemed somehow a little less certain.

Some Other Things I Especially Don't Like (Besides Rats)

"Lord, it is my chief complaint...."

– William Cowper –

nything that is supposed to be piping hot but actually is lukewarm ... anything that is supposed to be ice cold but actually is lukewarm ... people who ask questions but don't wait for answers ... people who like to talk most of all when somebody else is talking ... people who don't seem to know how to quit talking ... people who won't start talking ... loud music in open cars ... tailgaters ... tire squealers ... temper tantrums ... tank shirts ... sidewalk spitters ... almost any kind of spitters ... people who can't talk without spitting ... women who spit ... anybody who spits in an elevator ... sloppy drunks ... sloppy kisses, especially from strangers ... especially from strangers of the same sex ... dogs who bark all night ... dogs who chase cars ... dogs who chase joggers ... dogs who bite joggers ... dogs who drop their drawers and go to the bathroom in front of a jogger ... dogs who go to the bathroom on the dining room rug, especially when it's an oriental rug ... cats who jump up on the bed where I'm sleeping, especially *when* I'm sleeping ... cats who are indifferent except when hungry ... cats categorically because they're impossible to herd ... dogs who are cat killers ... weather forecasters who warn of partly cloudy conditions ... television happy talk ... music dubbed into regular news stories on television ... canned applause ... soap operas ... soft soap artists ... soap stuck to the bottom of the bathtub ... bread stuck to the top of the mouth ... applause in church ... jokes told in church ... belly laughs in church ... children who study their navels during Communion ... parents who go on praying while their children are misbehaving in church ... children who go to church and the circus and the World Series and spend all the time looking at the people behind them ... a grasshopper under my shirt in front ... a grasshopper under my shirt in back ... a grasshopper in my underwear, especially when I'm also in my underwear ... climbing to the top of a tobacco barn, even if I were able to climb to the top of a tobacco barn ... housing tobacco ... cutting tobacco, even if I could cut tobacco ... suckering tobacco ... topping tobacco ... chopping out tobacco ... chewing tobacco ... smoking tobacco ... people who evangelize and moralize about smoking tobacco ... wet matches ... limp handshakes ... women who won't dance close ... icy roads ... people who drive on icy roads as if they were dry roads ... troublesome cows, especially the ones that kick and break your arm ... bulls who roam ... anything that won't come when called (politely) ... anybody who thinks it's old fashioned or too southern or unreasonable to teach a child to say "yessir" and "nosir" and "yes, ma'am" and "no, ma'am" ... anybody who makes fun of an older person ... anybody who thinks discipline for children is cruel and inhumane punishment ... children who pitch fits in supermarkets ... children who kick elders on their shins ... children who take advantage of grandmothers ... children who lie to grandfathers ... grandmothers who whip up on disciplinarian fathers ... male chauvinists ... female chauvinists ... womanizers ... manizers ... teasers of every species, even the ones whose job it is to tease ... people who play God with anthills ... people who take the name of God in vain (except, maybe, after they've hit their thumb with a ball-peen hammer)...people who shake their fist at God (no matter how many times they've been hit on the thumb with a ball-peen hammer) ... people who misuse God for private gain ... liars ... cheats ... thieves ... snobs ... racial prejudice ... people who can't enjoy a perfectly splendid ethnic joke ... people who don't believe there is such a thing as a perfectly splendid ethnic joke ... people who don't like people because they believe there is such a thing as a perfectly splendid ethnic joke ... electronic ministers in general ... electronic ministers who return from the dead in particular

... any man of God who charges by the prayer ... loud street corner preachers ... sellers of cheap religious trinkets ... wire clothes hangers ... wooden clothes hangers that come unglued ... crowded closets ... moths ... mothballs ... sagging closet poles ... pants and shirts that play hide-and-seek in the crowded closet with the wire clothes hangers and the wooden clothes hangers that come unglued on the sagging closet pole where the moths dine hungrily despite the mothballs ... wives who get on your case for throwing dirty clothes in the bottom of the crowded closet with the wire clothes hangers, the wooden clothes hangers that come unglued, the sagging closet poles, the moths, and the mothballs ... looking for socks' mates ... wearing mismatched socks out of sheer desperation ... socks with holes in the toes ... socks with heels worn thin enough to let light shine through ... sharing toothbrushes with strangers ... sharing toothbrushes with children ... sharing toothbrushes with your wife on a regular basis ... sharing ice cream cones with anybody ... candy bars, too ... drinking out of the same pop bottle with fellow workers ... people who show off by popping the cap off a pop bottle with their teeth, spitting the cap on the ground, walking on it, and looking smug about it ... people who park their chewing gum behind their ear, left or right ... people who park their chewing gum under the nearest surface ... moldy bread ... sour milk ... eggs with red specks in the yellow ... a spot of any color on a new tie the first day it's worn ... ties that change in style from narrow to wide and back to narrow in the space of three years ... people who go to the eight-item supermarket express lane with 500 items ... checkout people who don't blink an eye when people come to the supermarket express line with 500 items ... sore losers ...arrogant winners ... nitpickers ... cockroaches ... ticks ... fleas ... flies ... people who pull wings off flies ... people who kill crickets ... bats ... snakes ... groundhogs, especially Punxsutawney Phil ... termites ... potato bugs ... corn borers ... tobacco worms ... braggarts ... whiners ... whisperers ... gossipers ... troublemakers ... mean-spiritedness ... twerps ... twinks ... snits ... people who can't or won't say thank you ... people who can't or won't say excuse me ... people who can't or won't say I'm sorry ... communists ... fascists ... people who don't believe in competition ... naysayers ... pessimists ... people who make fun of optimists...speeches that begin with jokes ... speeches filled with nothing but jokes ... people who make a career out of delivering one-liners and nothing much else ... people who tell me I ought to smile ... people who gush ... people who won't hush ... won't blush ... all slush ... car payments ... cars that quit the day after the last payment ... people who don't think pickup trucks are quite proper ... broken windshield wipers ... squeaking windshield wipers ... people who won't dim their lights out of sheer meanness ... automotive repair rip-offs ... dentists who hurt ... leaking roofs ... leaking shoes ... a scratch on the toe of a new shoe ... clock watchers ... expensive watches ... spare expensive watches ... clocks that ring on the hour, incorrectly ... fireworks from the fifth of July to the third of July ... people who won't take no for an answer ... people who say yes but really mean no ... my own inconsistencies ... my own shortcomings ... my own mistakes ... my own industrial-strength stupidity ... my own slights, however unintended ... my own procrastination ... my own indecision ... talking when I should be listening ... writing when I should be reading ... reading when I should be writing ... being awake when I should be sleeping ... sleeping when I should be awake ... damning when I should be praising ... praising when I don't mean it ... being introverted ... assuming too much ... not recognizing that there's more right about the world and the people in it than there is wrong about the world and the people in it ... journalists who think they know everything.

William Stamps

"Like a dog, he hunts in dreams."

– Alfred, Lord Tennyson –

The view on a mid-winter morning through the frosted panes of the windows of this old house built to last centuries is one of hope that the cold weather we've needed has finally come. We'd been slogging through mud up to our shinbones since Christmas. The wool on the sheep has looked more like shabby throw rugs dredged through the muck. We and they have been pacing ourselves because it serves no purpose to be in a hurry when navigating swamps. We incline our heads in the direction we're going and try to keep from sinking much past our knees.

We know of some who've headed off for Florida, as has become their habit; but many of us remain at the homeplace in Kentucky through each of the days of the seasons, the coldest and balmiest, maybe because we consider it our duty. Or we simply have a stubborn streak that's rewarded with the knowledge that we've earned spring. Either way, like sentries loyal to our posts, we've committed ourselves to the seasonal values and vagaries of the commonwealth.

The sheep have been culling themselves, helped along by our "no pampering" policy. You could bring the sheep inside the parlor and treat them to afternoon tea, and they would still find an excuse to bargain for "the great goodnight." Since there's little if anything to be gained by loading up muddy, bedraggled throw rugs and hauling them off to market, we give them all the time they think they need to wallow deeper into the mud and sink to their own oblivions.

One day, at the Institution of Higher Learning, a young woman with her gender engines revved to about 80 rpm, informed me that what the ewes ought to do down on Plum Lick was to go on strike. She said, the ewes ought to stand up for their rights and tell the rams, "Hell no, we aren't going to breed."

I tried to explain to her that it probably wouldn't work, because the rams would likely go off somewhere else and look for something else to do. The young woman looked at me, I thought, with a certain sadness that there was no hope that I would ever be nurtured into the mainstream of gender sensitivities.

Which brings me to William Stamps, the arthritic black and tan coonhound who last year roused himself, broke into the shop, shouldered aside the intended sire for our Australian shepherd, Pumpkin, and bred her to a fair *three* well. He's spending his new year sleeping in the side yard, looking for rays of sunshine and possibly wondering if there might have been a connection between his new super-relaxed comfort index and the last trip he took to the vet's office.

Jeanne, our only half-breed Australian shepherd/coonhound that looks like her mother, is the sweetest of the gang of three. Her tail is docked, which sets her apart from her sisters. They and their long-tailed way of looking at things resent all the special attention bestowed upon Jeanne. They snarl in her face and bite her on the end of the nose at feeding time. What they don't understand is that they, as their father, William Stamps, will be stopped in their genetic tracks while Jeanne, lightly touched by the magic lady's sparkling wand, will become Cinderella for Chip, the princely border collie. That is, unless some stranger hound in the night picks up the scent and hightails it into our place.

This relates rather directly to a conversation I had with a

J. LARKINS

breeder of Australian shepherds in Wilkinson County, Mississippi.

"John," I said to my friend John Hewes, "If a bitch in heat is out there with you and she is working cattle, and six dogs come over the hill, what will happen? Will the bitch keep on working cattle?"

John replied, rather soberly I thought: "She'll breed."

"Well then, what do you do?" I asked.

"I shoot the six dogs," he said.

Which brings us to tomatoes. A long way around, but here we are. We heard yet another report recently about genetically controlled tomatoes. At mid-winter we think there's a difference between this and dogs. Maybe. Fine-tuning the breed of a dog is one thing; manipulating the flavor of a tomato strikes us at best as a dubious piece of business. It just seems to us that the heart and soul of vine-ripened tomatoes is the short walk from the kitchen to the garden to gather them in and gamble on the flavor. First thing you know, somebody will come up with genetically controlled love. In this arrangement nobody would ever have to worry, because we'd be programmed to hook up with exactly the right person for all seasons, for as long as we live. We might fix it so we could live forever, too. The flavor would be perfect, and there would be no breakups. Of course, a lot of attorneys, ministers, marriage counselors, soap opera producers, and gender research teaching assistants would have to find something else to do. They might even work on their own love for one another. Heavens.

Call it cabin fever. Call it staring through frosted panes of window glass in an old house that should have been torn down a long time ago and replaced with plastics. Call it whatever you will, it's how we're spending a winter day on Plum Lick—as naturally and as disorganized as possible with the exception of William Stamps, doggone his coondog hide. He had to go and push his luck too far one too many times and now has nothing to look forward to but snoring through another summer.

Another thing: is it too much to hope that those television forecasters get it straight once and for all that sunshine doesn't hold a monopoly on "good," and frozen-hard ground isn't necessarily bad? Gimme a break. We need an honest-to-goodness, snow-on-the-ground, below-zero-reading-on-the-back-porch, fire-building, human-snuggling winter so we can have a spring worthy of the name. When are they going to understand that? Probably never. Unless we legislate the rascal weather forecasters, or manipulate their genes.

Goats and Purple Martins

"That man is the richest whose pleasures
are the cheapest."
– Henry David Thoreau –

About six miles east of Maysville on KY 10, up the hill from the head of Bull Creek, through the community of Plumville is where Jimmy and Wilma Williams live. Jimmy trains goats to pull wagons loaded with children. It's kind of funny to see people's reactions when a wagon pulled by goats heads in their direction. It's generally an occasion for smiles. For Jimmy, who's been using goats to pull things since he was 14 years old, it produces some money but mostly satisfaction now that he's going to be 64 years old this year. Fifty years can make a man turn to goats and pretty much stick with them.

"It's not a big money-making thing...we do it just because we love it," says Jimmy, sitting in the coolness of his side porch on a lazy late summer Sunday afternoon. Jimmy's goats (Saanens, Toggenburgs, and French Alpines) seem to *want* to pull wagons filled with children because the goats love it too. Or they love Jimmy, and whatever he wants is what they want.

"They love to do it...they know when I put the big collar on them and open up the gate they go straight to the trailer and to their own stall."

Everybody at the Salt Lick Homecoming or the Morehead Harvest festivals this year saw Jimmy and the Toggenburg pair—Tom and Jerry—pulling "kids" at a dollar a ride. Those goats had as much character as Clydesdales, and Tom and Jerry looked as majestically poised in their harness as horses in a Sugar Bowl commercial. One thing about Jimmy and Wilma—they don't work the goats too long on Saturdays, and never on Sundays. Jimmy and Wilma attend church across the Mason County line in Wallingford, which is in Fleming County.

The French Alpine pair, Jim and Jeff, and the Saanen pair, Chip and Dale, and the spare goat, who else but Randy, enjoy their Sundays off too. But they don't mind coming to the gate to visit with a stranger. Each with his bell ringing (all of them ringing loudly at the same time tells Jimmy there's a dog inside the electric fence), these goats are friendly to a fault, or a goatee. True, they like to nibble at a stranger's pant leg, and, yes, the French Alpines might make a visitor think the short, sharp horns are about to come a little too close to the groin for comfort, but the way the goats take to Jimmy is good for the soul. Restores faith in peace at the center.

"They're just like babies," says Jimmy as his hand cups around Chip's face (or was it Dale?). "They depend on me to tell 'em where to go...keep 'em straight...do what I want 'em to do."

"Here, shake hands with me," says Jimmy to one of the French Alpines, and Jim (or was it Jeff?) sticks out a leg for shaking. When Jimmy Williams was growing up in Lewis County, he trained goats to pull firewood to the house.

"What about billy goats?"

"Never keep 'em."

"I've heard they smell real bad."

"You can smell 'em from here to way over there past that purple martin house," says Jimmy.

"Do goats eat tin cans?"

"Had a woman ask me that once. I said 'look at his mouth.'"

"Why, he doesn't have any teeth on top," said the woman.

"Can you imagine a goat eatin' a tin can?" Jimmy asked her.

When they retire, Jimmy and Wilma would like to travel up to the Amish country of Pennsylvania or the Blue Ridge Mountains or maybe go down to Nashville to visit the Grand Ole Opry. Or they might just stay home in Kentucky. But for now, when Jimmy's not carpentering for an insurance company, they love to pull children in a homemade goat wagon; it doesn't matter if it's a birthday party, a day care center, or a vacation Bible school. Summer festivals in Kentucky are special fun.

"Look at those goats pulling that wagon! Look at those red hats they're wearing!"

"Can I ride too, Mister?"

"Cost you $1," says Jimmy.

Sometimes, if a "kid" doesn't have a dollar, Jimmy will say: "Jump up on this wagon."

"Jimmy, do you ever wonder about that expression, 'separating the sheep from the goats,' as if to say, sheep are good, but goats are bad?"

"Yep," says Jimmy with a shy and knowing smile.

The telephone rang, and it was Jimmy talking.

"I want to do something nice for you."

"Why that's mighty nice, Jimmy, what is it?"

"You remember when you were up here last year, and we were sitting there talking, and you admired my martin house?"

"Yessir."

"Well, I'm going to build you one."

"My goodness."

"It'll have 16 rooms and I'll paint it any color you want it."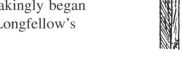

"Jimmy, that's about the nicest thing anybody's ever done for me, and I want you to know how much I appreciate it."

"No problem."

Jimmy Williams went to work as the winter of 1993-1994 piled snow 25 inches deep around his shop on the edge of Plumville in Mason County. The temperature plummeted to 30 below zero, but the big stove in Jimmy's shop kept him warm as he painstakingly began cutting the wood to build one of Longfellow's "half-way houses on the way to heaven!"

The dimensions were precise, and the work proceeded accordingly: 16 rooms—each six inches in, six inches across, six inches high, with individual entrances two-and-one-half inches in diameter. The holes were slightly higher than the recommended one inch up from the floor.

"I've had trouble with the babies falling out," said Jimmy, so he's begun raising the holes a trifle to try to prevent disasters.

Next, he built an air shaft through the center of the apartment house, and he constructed vents under the eaves of the roof, which he made from metal so as to give a nice sound on rainy nights, although birds might not take on so about this sort of thing the way some humans do out in the country.

"What color did you say you'd like for it to be?" Jimmy wanted to know.

"How about white with a green roof?" That's the color of our house, and I thought it would look nice if the birds had the same decoration.

"Done."

Jimmy was waiting for me in his shop at Plumville on the Ides of March, the birthday of my wife, who from this day forward would be connected in my mind with the return of the purple martins. I got to thinking, if she precedes me, I'll feel her presence with the annual reappearance of the blue-black birds from Latin America, where she and I once worked. Should I precede her, she would witness the arrival of the first swallows and remember how our lives always hinged on hope.

In the words of James Fisher and Roger Tory Peterson: "No philosophers they, they live and die in a drama of colors and shapes and music that makes philosophers of us."

Jimmy helped me load the purple martin house into the front seat of the car. It was a tight fit with no room to spare.

"Well, Jimmy, I suppose our paths will cross many times this year at the community festivals."

"Oh, yes."

"Will you be bringing Tom and Jerry again to pull the wagon for the children?"

"No. Jerry died of pneumonia this winter past, and Tom, he's not well."

"I'm sorry. Then, who'll be the team of goats this year?"

"It'll be the Saanens, Chip and Dale. Randy will be the spare. They're all ready to go." Later, Jimmy said there'd also be Jim and Jeff, and probably a new Tom and Jerry.

"So long, Jimmy...I'm on my way home."

Jimmy made me promise to sneak his telephone number into the next thing I wrote about him—(606) 564-9812—shhhhhhhh: I told him the editor would probably throw it out, but Jimmy whispered, "I hope not."

Cousin Marvin and Reda came over and helped us raise our new purple martin house on Plum Lick to a height of about 14 feet above the ground on a six-by-six post. Jimmy had said to be sure to locate it away from trees, because the martins don't prefer to share their perching with every Tom, Dick, and Harry.

On March 25, about two-dozen swallows returned to Jimmy's house at Plumville, but here on Plum Lick we are still looking at what appear to be mixed sparrows and ugly starlings. I guess we can't blame the purple martins. How were they supposed to know?

Jimmy said that when his flock arrived they ran the other birds off. Maybe next year our purple martin house will be listed with the better travel agencies down south.

PART TWO

Remembrance

Dad

"You will find yourself a partner in the
Glory of the Garden."

– Rudyard Kipling –

*D*ad's tomatoes and peppers, the heart of his garden, were in their mid-summer glory, glistening with early morning moisture. There were onion and garlic sets, potatoes, sweet basil, squash, celery, carrots, radishes, curly endive, bib lettuce, green beans, and four rows of yellow sweet corn, and popcorn (sometimes), but it was the tomatoes and the peppers, especially the peppers, that possessed Dad's psyche. There were bell peppers and banana peppers and miniature red hot peppers and hotter jalapeño peppers. Life without peppers was not Dad's idea of a life worth living.

I called him Dad out of respect, although he was not my father, but my father-in-law. "Dad" was an expression as natural for me as the first intelligible sounds made by babies, and I liked calling him "Dad," because it seemed to connect me with a life force I'd not been able to remember before in the same way. Even though he'd not come out to California for my wedding with his daughter, Rose, I had hungered for the first time when I would see the strong-willed Sicilian, who would leave a permanent mark on me.

He taught me nothing from books. There was no great literature in his house. He probably shook his head in bewilderment and perhaps distrust that a son-in-law would care so much about *books*. Instead, by his example, Dad taught me to love and respect the soil. He caused me to know with more certainty than I'd ever experienced before the value of all that grows from the good earth, and he did not need to read Pearl Buck to understand such a fundamental truth.

Each evening when he watered his ten rows of peppers, Dad did it "scientifically," wrapping the end of the garden hose with a small piece of white cloth, inserting the end of the covered tube inside an empty, clay, flower pot, spreading the water through the hole in the bottom, evenly and smoothly, protecting the plants already burdened with large, sweet fruit awaiting the picking and the roasting on the backyard grill, or in Mom's kitchen, the cooking in olive oil ordered up from Kansas City or over from Chicago.

Life without olive oil for cooking was not Mom's idea of a life in the fullest sense of the meaning either. She and Dad lived to eat, as all good Sicilians should and did and would until the priest arrived to administer final rites—*"En nomine Patri, y Filis, y Spiritus Sancti"*—it had been that way in the old days in Italy, and the seeds of tradition of garden and kitchen would travel with Frank and Mary on their separate voyages to the New World.

Mom and her mother disembarked on May 1, 1921, in the Battery Park neighborhood of Brooklyn and four days later, after passing through the Ellis Island nightmare, they would be on a train headed for St. Joseph, Missouri, where Mom's brother lived. Mom was 18 years old, the picture of health and enthusiasm for starting her new life in the amazing United States of America.

Dad had preceded Mom to America by ten years, when he was 16 years old. He had taken the train to Centerville, Iowa, to join his father and brother in the coal mining industry. Since he didn't believe in debt and not in his lifetime would he pay for anything with plastic money, Dad needed ten years to prepare for his proper marriage to Mom on October 27, 1923. It was two years after her arrival—she was 20 years old, and he was 28—when they sank their roots into the black loam of southeastern Iowa.

They had come with hardly more than the clothes they wore—a mite of pin money inside Mom's blouse, a tight and twisted wad of lire in Dad's formless trousers hanging from the wide leather belt, the main support for covering legs upon which he would stand on his own, not looking for handouts, not wanting handouts. Dad was a republican.

"Those gotdam democrats—hey, what you think, Davie?" he'd roar and jab me in the ribs during the later years, whenever the subject of politics would come back to haunt him from what he perceived to be the dark days of the Franklin Delano Roosevelt administrations of the 1930s. If there were anyone Dad had despised and distrusted more than FDR, it was Mrs. FDR. And if there were anyone he detested more than she, it was the young punk of a military officer sent out to the mine with orders for Dad to fly the American Flag during World War II. It had been a silly intrusion, and Dad was very choosy about who walked up the long steps to the top of the elevator shaft, because that's where the controls were, and *nobody* put their gotdam hands on the controls except the man who had bought and paid for the gotdam thing.

Dad had survived the Great Depression on the strength of his own two legs, his broad shoulders, and arms with those hands of steely grip, a young coal miner searching for his own deep shaft. In order to *earn* that right, first he'd work the railroads, sweating long hours for pennies in the laying of steel, the driving of spikes from Ellis Island to West Virginia, dipping cold biscuits in the soup of railroad yard vats, drinking strong coffee, squeezing the eagle until it screamed, rubbing his huge, darkening thumb with its splintered, crusted nail over the Lincoln-head pennies and the Indian-head nickels, saving his pennies and nickels, thinking of them as soldiers in his personal army, according each one greatest respect as he labored in the prime of his youth from West Virginia through Ohio and Indiana to Springfield, Illinois, westward to Iowa.

Mom's teenage years in America included long days and nights earning her own pennies and nickels in the sewing factories of Chicago. Even after Dad had saved enough to stake out his dream of a small coal mine in Appanoose County, Iowa, and after he had laid enough by to propose marriage to the young girl who'd left her homeland back in Sicily, even then she'd gone to Chicago to help make shirts for the dandies who drank prohibition gin and danced the Charleston, and she made clothes for government functionaries sent out to solve with federal programs the problems of society.

"Gotdam welfare—what you think, Davie?" and my father-in-law would jab me in the ribs again. I'd smile, but words always failed me. There was no way—I mean, it wasn't in me to outtalk him, and so I didn't even want to try. Whenever I went out to the mine, I kept a respectful distance from Dad, because it would be a little like visiting with the pilot in the cockpit of a jumbo jet about to land. In the same way, there was no talking to Dad when he was operating the elevator at the top of the main shaft of the mine.

His partner, Padino, worked with the miners beneath the surface, and talking to Padino down there was like talking to somebody's co-pilot during an instrument landing. You didn't talk to Padino. You listened to Padino. Padino and Dad had an amazingly stable love-hate relationship, and it was a good arrangement to have them separated during working hours. In their off time, their neighboring gardens were separated by a small swath of grass where next generations played tag football, never dreaming of mining coal, finding their life's experiences stimulated and mirrored by television beamed down from Des Moines.

Mom and Padina, who in their turn would become matriarchs by default, were close as sisters, and they didn't mind showing it. They didn't compete the way Dad and Padino did over the mining of coal and the growing of gardens. I don't remember ever seeing Dad inside Padino's house, and I don't remember ever seeing Padino inside Dad's house. It was a turf thing. Were you to ask about it, you'd hear low, menacing growls.

The Big Boys, the red and the yellow, and the teardrop-shaped tomatoes, were clustered on the firm vines growing horizontally as well as vertically on the wooden supports Dad had constructed, stored, and brought out each spring after the last of another punishing Iowa winter when just getting to and from the mine in the old, snub-nosed pickup truck, weaving through the caverns of snowbanks, was in and of itself a daily test of strength and determination. Dad's coldest days of winter were spent atop the tipple, raising up riches measured in potential warmth as well as dollars. For Dad and Padino, spring was a blessed resurrection, although they would never speak of it in that way.

Each tomato niño had begun as a seed in a tray four inches deep, 24 inches long, and 11 inches wide, and had been prepped by the sun coming through the basement windows of the house Dad had built for his bride and the six children who'd follow. Maybe, praise God, one of them would choose to live there and continue the tradition of the peppers and the tomatoes, the fennel seed, the sausage, the homemade bread, and the homemade red wine from the Zampatella and the Muscat grapes ordered from California. But, of course, there would need to be encouragement for the children to stay, some urging for them not to move out to California, down to Kansas or up to Minnesota. In fairness to each, there would be father-and-son, mother-and-daughter pressures, so that continuity was not likely to move past fantasy.

Mom managed two kitchens, one on the ground floor of the six-room house at 525 E. Walnut Street in Centerville, Iowa. The second of Mom's kitchens was downstairs in the basement, shared with Dad's and Padino's spare parts for the mine. Nothing of value was thrown away or traded in by Dad and Mom; everything that could be saved was used: a stand-up freezer in the basement, a combination refrigerator/freezer upstairs, a newer gas stove by the side of the family eating table, an older, antique gas oven downstairs. There was an old sewing machine in the corner of the kitchen upstairs, where Mom made clothes for her children and her children's children, and from time to time she would make something new for herself, and she'd proudly wear it to Mass on Sunday.

The spaghetti sauce was made first thing in the morning and almost always there were special platefuls of spaghetti on Sundays.

"While Mom went to church I would stir it for her," Rose, the second child remembered. "Dad loved to put hot pepper from the garden in the sauce when Mom was not looking. But he knew he would get in trouble, because she didn't want the sauce that hot."

Rose inherited Mom's sweeter, quieter genes, and when Rose bore her own four children, she bequeathed to them her mother's patience and forgiveness. Rose did not remarry after our divorce, becoming a devoted grandmother, and accepting her name, "Grandma Rose," with grace, she showered affection upon her progeny.

When Dad bought the brand new Dodge sedan in the '40s, he paid $3,000 for it, and he was proud that every penny was in cash.

"It was a beautiful maroon, and the chrome made the car just outstanding," Rose remembered with deep pleasure begotten of Dad's decision that she should have the honor of formal driving lessons.

The heavily framed black and white picture of Mom and Dad and their 1923 wedding party hung in the living room through much of the 20th century, but in time, even in their youth, the shy, self-conscious faces would seem much older to Rose, the other five children, 19 grandchildren, and 26 great-grandchildren. In all their veins would flow original Sicilian blood, and there would be strength in the youth of their individualism, a blazing heat in their hearts to create new and meaningful lives in the United States, an opportunity for some, at least, for lasting peace at the center.

Sausage-making was a central part of the days of the life of the family, Mom walking to the grocery to buy pork shoulder, bringing it home, and cutting it into small pieces to be fed into the grinder clamped to the round table in the middle of the basement kitchen. She also bought casings, the cleaned and preserved hog intestines, which she carefully fitted over the steel cone of the grinder. She turned the wooden handle with her right hand, feeding the seasoned cuts of meat into the top of the grinder with her left hand, which she also used to keep the casing snug on the cone as the meat came through, emerging as long, looping coils of homemade Italian sausage.

Dad grew fennel on the edge of his garden, the pungent seeds of the European plant with its small yellow flowers pre-destined to become a dominant flavor in the sausage piling higher on Mom's basement table, the same table where she kneaded her bread, first in the large bowl and then out on the table itself, loaves of bread baked golden brown on top, soft as angel food cake in the middle. In the large bowl she measured out five pounds of flour, and she put in yeast that had been mixed with warm water.

"She mixed this and put a towel on top and set it in a very warm place to rise. When it was ready to be put into loaves, she would take a certain amount and make about six or seven loaves," Rose would remember, and Mom would put oil on top of each loaf so it would brown. She would make small rolls too, and if it were necessary on that day, she would use some of the dough to make pizza. There was magic in Mom's touch, yet her daughters were not as possessed with the desire to immerse their hands in the dough, to feel the fine, sifted flour on their fingertips—perhaps they found it faster, easier, more modern to buy bread at the store and pizza at the carryout window. If they had truly *wanted* to bake bread at home they would have, but times change and the art of baking bread in one family would doubtless die when Mom did, and the same outcomes were unfolding next door in Padino and Padina's house.

Dad followed several procedures as religiously as he attended early Mass on Sunday: pinch off all lower stems on the tomato plants, ruthlessly snap out all suckers wherever and whenever they appeared in order to strengthen the main stems; harvest vegetables early in the morning, when freshness was at its peak; water the peppers daily and carefully from the cistern he had dug when the house was built, disregarding all town-imposed "water hours" during dry spells; and humor his grandchildren up to the edge of the garden but not one step beyond it.

"John!" (he called all small children, girls and boys, "John"): "Go see you mamma."

"But, Grandpa..."

"You mamma's callin' *you!*" he would boom.

Dad was as death on children in his garden as Mr. McGregor was with errant, foolish Peter Rabbits. Children were every bit as dangerous as rabbits in Dad's garden and just as incompatible. He was *serious* about his garden, for without his garden Dad was the same as a man without clothes to wear, without stories to tell at a table filled with skillet-smothered sausage, Mom's homemade bread, and the California wine home-made in Iowa to smooth the digestion and build up the blood.

"Here, you taka spoonful! See? Itsa good for heem!"

After the shipment arrived from California, Dad placed bunches of what were now his own private fruit of angels inside a grape press, and when they were ready he put pulp and juice in an open barrel to let it all ferment a week to ten days. He added sugar when the fermentation was slow. Next, the fermented liquid was run through the juice press, leaving the lovely, frothy liquid to pour into sealed, oak-staved barrels, each with a tightly fitted wooden spigot. Dad kept three 50-gallon barrels working in the rear of the basement pantry, one just started, one almost ready and one just right for the filling of smaller kegs to go upstairs to be near the table for the daily feasts, the pouring of the glasses for everybody and—teaspoonfuls for the very young "Johns."

"Salud!"

"Salud!"

"Salud!"

Arms went out at 45-degree angles around the table. And there was the clinking of glasses.

For Dad, time, all experience, all feeling and caring and loyalty lay within the framework of his immediate family, not in the family of his forefathers, nor directly in families as yet unborn, but within that circle of children who gathered around his table where the taking of meals replaced all other activities. He pounded his fist on the table, speared the sliced tomatoes, jabbed sons-in-law in their ribs, squeezed Mom's sloping shoulder, drank his wine in great gulps, and stomped his right foot with the joy that comes to a man who has tended his garden well and seen its fruits appear before him for rites of consummation.

Dad and Mom did not eat in restaurants. It would be unthinkable to leave one's own table for an artificial setting, and anyway, there was no food cooked as well and with as much love as Mom's. Birthdays and Santa Clauses became times of considerably awkward embarrassment. In fact, anything commercially institutionalized, anything except the home and the Church, were someone else's business, questionable business at that. Dad and Mom were original tribal elders, and it would be unnatural to forsake or supplant the fundamental responsibility of the garden for growing, the kitchen for cooking, and the bed for procreating future generations.

The day finally came, as he must have known it would, when Dad realized he had no choice but to close the mine. He and Padino had seen the cost of production soar, the hiring of labor become increasingly difficult, and the market for coal shipped on the Burlington and Rock Island Lines fall victim to the efficiencies as well as the destructiveness of strip mining. Anyway, the two men's muscles and minds were wearing down like the once strong, tough-willed miniature ponies that year after year pulled the carts over the subterranean tracks, summer and winter.

At Padino's funeral, Dad sat nearby and talked directly to his old friend:

"He wasn't sick. There wasn't anything wrong with heem. He was all right. He wasn't sick."

"Hail Mary, full of grace," the rosary began with Padina in her grief, even though Dad would not stop insisting, "He wasn't sick. There wasn't anything wrong with heem."

Padino *had* been sick. He'd simply not complained about the gassing in World War I that had deeply scarred his lungs for life. Yet Padino's was a tough little Sicilian body that had tolerated the damage until at the age of 83 he had contracted pneumonia, his heart had greatly enlarged, and he had died on his son Michael's 40th birthday.

"He had been up at six o'clock every morning for his shot of wine," said Mike, who would always remember on each of his birthday anniversaries, the date of his father's death.

On that day, July 7, 1975, a sleeping killer had not yet awakened in Dad, and as he sat by the side of Padino's coffin, he could not know that in seven years his own death would finally come to pass. Cancer would be born in him as it would be in tens of thousands of other men and women in the United States, and it would specifically stalk most males by invading the walnut-sized prostate gland in that part of the body so exalted and jealously guarded by its master. It came so quietly that Dad would not understand the beginnings of discomfort in his lower back when he would bend down in early mornings to gather in fresh vegetables from his garden. During the night, he would interpret the frequent trips to the bathroom as surely nothing more nor less than a sign of advancing years, a restlessness having more to do, he imagined, with the selling of the mine and the ponies and the equipment than it did with something as small and private and personal as a body gland closing like a fist around his urethra, the gland becoming as hard as a deeply-ridged black walnut.

Prostate cancer would overtake me too, in what would come to be known as the epidemic of prostate cancer in 1994. As there would be trips to the hospital in Cedar Rapids, Iowa, for Dad in the 1980s, there would be trips to the hospital in Lexington, Kentucky, for me in the 1990s. The doctors and the nurses tried to alleviate the pain of Dad's spreading cancer, but in his voice on the telephone the last time to me in those terminal, awkward, and embarrassing years after the divorce from Rose, there had been an unfamiliar tone in the utterance, strange and desperate, devoid of the passion that had made Dad such an awesome power. The thunder that had rolled out of the East from Ellis Island across the American Midwest to a coal mine and a garden in southeastern Iowa had weakened to a whisper.

At Dad's funeral, September 18, 1982, Mom, in her 79th year, handed individual roses to each of the grandsons, and they in turn placed them, with their hands of softness, one by one, on the coffin before it was lowered into the dark soil of Dad's new world.

His legacy for his children, grandchildren, and great-grandchildren was a seed of knowledge that the patriarch, who had come over from

Calascibetta, Sicily, had lived as good a life as any native-born American, had done it with his own hands, believing entirely in himself, never once asking what his country could do for him, living, "Praise Got, Davie," long enough to see a Catholic elected President of the United States (never mind that he was a democrat).

Mom, the matriarch in her 90th year in 1994, might wonder as she went to sleep each night, why the solid, brick house on East Walnut Street would no longer echo with the shouts of her children, would remain strangely silent. She might also dream of what Dad would think if he could see the grass sod growing where once had been his garden.

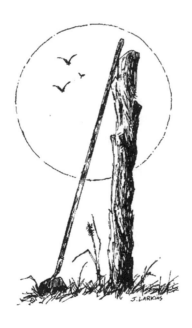

My Three Dads

"...they withered all when my father died."

– William Shakespeare –

$\mathcal{I}$ have had the good fortune to have had three fathers, as well as "Dad," who for 25 years was my father-in-law. Each gave me lessons for a lifetime. My only regret is that I am sending them Father's Day flowers too late.

Samuel was my natural father, but I do not remember ever having seen his face, or having heard the sound of his voice. We were both, he and I, young when he died—he was 36 years old, and I was 18 months old. I was always told that he had a marvelous tenor voice. Sam could sing and make an audience cry. One time, his sister, my Aunt Florence, decided I should have the small disc upon which was a recording of my father singing. Aunt Florence had always said one of his favorites was "Just a Song at Twilight." I took the disc to a record shop where I believed I would listen as an adult for the first time to my father's voice. I remember how excited I was. The disc was placed on the turntable, the needle carefully placed upon the first groove. I will never know what happened: there was *nothing* on the disc, except the soft scratch of the needle, the disc turning silently around the pin in the center.

"Just a Song at Twilight" may be a piece of simple sentimentality, but whenever I hear it, I think of the young doctor, my father Samuel, who had the son he always wanted, and for 18 months was able to sing him to sleep at night. The son's not being able to remember would not matter so much as the singing:

"Rockabye Baby, in the tree top..."

After my father died and was buried next to his parents, Nellie and Coleman, I was "farmed out" to a childless couple, Bob and E, the two lovely people who knew more about peace at the center than I.

My third father was "Mr. Bill," my mother's second husband. He was not a finder of marbles, nor a carver of peach-seed baskets, nor a black-walnut creator like Bob, nor a romantic like Samuel. "Mr. Bill" was too intent on perpetuating Mt. Auburn, his ancestral home, too realistic, too practical for such games. Even though the antebellum mansion in the passage of time has passed to other outside families, from "Mr. Bill" I learned important lessons, and they stuck in my brain amid Samuel's music and Bob's illusions.

"Never is a helluva long time, Son."

"Always remember, no matter how good you think you are at anything, there's always somebody else who's a little bit better."

"The early bird gets the worm."

"Get a good education, Son, because that's something NOBODY can take away from you."

The first time he and I turned down the Plum Lick Road in his pickup truck, when I was about 14 years old, Mr. Bill said to me: "You may live here one day, Son."

At that time, I did not thank him, because I was too young and I didn't understand the meaning of the trip we were taking from the big house into the backwoods on the other side of the watershed. Soon I would learn from Mr. Bill that he was divorcing my mother, and now in 1994, each time I turn down the Plum Lick Road, I remember the words:

"You may live here one day, Son."

Now I say aloud, "Thank you, Mr. Bill."

He is gone. Bob is gone. And Samuel is gone. Yet in a very real way they are not gone at all. I see them and hear them upon the singing of certain songs, during the playing of certain games, and when I speak with certain students, including my own children.

My three dads are living their spiritual lives, through me, in part—and they make me better by their presence.

Bob

> "The noblest works and foundations have proceeded
> from childless men, which have sought to express
> the images of their minds where those of their
> bodies have failed."
>
> **– Francis Bacon –**

*B*ob positioned the black walnut in the vise and tightened down. The greying vision was shaded by arching clumps of hairs on his brow above eyes becoming milky with the heap of years—his three score and ten—with tears hanging on the corners of his eyes, appearing there not to foretell crying, but as the wateriness of weary lingering on the outer edge of living.

Bob was born on Flag Day, and each Flag Day he would smile and say the flags were flying for him. Bob was very shy and soft-spoken. If he were ever to yell, it would take the last ounce of energy in his body, a bending frame becoming more frail, with each year becoming more difficult than the one preceding. He suffered from asthma most of his life, wheezing so much it drove Lida, his wife, to considerable distraction.

Bob leaned down closer to the vise, gripped the long steel lever to pinion the walnut perfectly in alignment for the cutting, cleared his throat carefully, not wanting to trigger too soon the asthma racking his lungs each of these final days. He reached for the hacksaw poised on the wooden peg above his workbench.

In his youth, Bob had been a carpenter's carpenter, knowing with deep satisfaction the value of nails driven without bending, saws lightly oiled and returned to their beds for sleeping, the right screwdriver for the right screw thread, the nature of wood and how each variety could best be used. He was a blacksmith, too, but born

30 years too late, a gentle spirit for whom the bellows fanned a fire less needed. He shoed the last of the dwindling population of work horses in the vicinity of the house where he was born, repaired wagon singletrees, which soon were to become antique wall hangings, married Lida, and moved to town to wait for the tolling of bells. "Lida" or "Lide" was shortened to "E" by a neighbor child, and it stuck for the rest of her life. She was always just plain "E."

Despite her mostly feigned frustrations, "E" helped Bob all she could. In time, he became her child and she scolded him every waking moment. Hardly anybody called him "Robert," but she called him "Rob," and when she said his name she varied the sound of the "R" and the "b" to suit her mood, almost always snappish. "E" became a shrew, the rough exterior, the scowl, the tartness of her words belying a heart of gold, feelings so fragile it would be just awful to see her convulse with hurt.

"E" burned sulfur in mayonnaise jar lids and set them on the edge of the upstairs wash basin almost every night, especially on hot summer nights so that Bob could sit on the closed commode seat and lean over with his head supported by his left hand on his forehead, his right hand on his right knee for balance, breathing the yellow, astringent fumes into his lungs. It never seemed to work very well.

Bob went on wheezing until "E" knew there was no other choice but to give him the "hypo," the shot instantly producing the relief he desperately needed. It could have been morphine. Whatever it was, it was potent. After the needle was withdrawn and "E" had sighed and shaken her head, Bob lay his head on his pillow and slept like a baby.

"Now I lay me down to sleep, I pray the Lord my soul to keep; if I die before I wake, I pray the Lord my soul to take." It was the prayer Bob said each night with each of his foster children. Sometimes, one of the children would say the prayer for Bob, because he was too weak to say it, and the child would smooth back the thinning hair on his forehead.

Bob—some of his nieces and nephews called him "Uncle Bobert—always seemed distant from the center of things, especially those matters others considered to be of major importance. For a long time, there was no telephone in the house. There was never a television set. The only book in the house was the Bible. When Bob moved to the center of something he truly cared about, such as cutting open black walnuts to make necklace pieces of them, it became a project only his hands felt with a soft, sure, and loving touch, so intimate as to warrant embarrassment for him when other eyes watched.

Bob and "E" were childless but their six-room house at 1841 South Main Street became a kind of foster home for many who were almost always well and smiling, while others were regularly in sickly condition, bringing out "E's" natural nursing gift. She spent hours by the bedside of a little boy with double pneumonia, administered the sulfa drug, listened each morning to determine the rise and the fall of the rasping, took his temperature and reassured him so as not to worry as each "four o'clock fever" rolled around.

When Bob, who sat in a rocking chair on the other side of the room, used the small whetstone he kept inside its original box, he'd take it out slowly, removing the velvet sleeve as carefully as a big city man would recall hands from kid gloves. He'd sit in his rocking chair, spit on the stone, spreading the saliva back and forth with the edge of the glistening knife blade, buttering it more carefully than he would one of "E's" big oven-brown biscuits.

Bob hardly ever talked. He let "E" and others babble to their heart's content. Bob sometimes called "E" "Now Sweet," generally drawing from her a frown sealing off the last of any secret seductiveness sleeping in her aging body. She didn't miss a day using Bob as a sounding board, some would say it was more like a punching bag with a constant cannonade of words. They were words spoken only in the house and nowhere else because late in her life, "E" seldom went outside and rarely left the yard. Bob heard the words, many of them sharp, some almost venomous, and though he surely must've heard them all, he never let on, because he knew if he answered back, "E" would cry and that was something he couldn't bear. When "E" heaped abuse on him, Bob centered down deeper into his detachment from everything around him, and he kept sharpening his knife.

He used his knife to carve out peach-seed baskets when he wasn't hacksawing black walnuts, as a jeweler would work. Bob couldn't have been happier if he had been cutting diamonds and polishing pearls. Peach seeds and black walnuts were two of his main loves, and he certainly thought more of them than any gems dug up in some foreign land, shipped across the water, bought and sold many times to be finally twisted into expensive costume doohickies.

Bob's peach-seed baskets and black-walnut sections were not for sale, the way his soul was not on the market. Like Thoreau, a man Bob never knew because he was too busy at work with his hands in his own Walden to read books, Bob could also have said, "...instead of studying how to make it worth men's while to buy my baskets, I studied rather how to avoid the necessity of selling them." Bob could have said that. If he were in the habit of talking.

When Bob finished one peach-seed basket or black-walnut design he'd start another, then another, and another until he had enough for a necklace of miniature baskets and black-walnut patterns, each piece polished and varnished to preserve the sheath, the outer garment of the seed, the center of creation, a fitting gift for a little girl who admired it. Or, the black-walnut sections might become large buttons for bright sweaters.

Polished and varnished, the intricate intertwinements of the black-walnut configurations were as durable as freshly minted silver half-dollars. For Bob, the annual production of Black Walnut trees was by far more valuable in real terms than the production of the nation's mints, peach seeds more lovely than mere emeralds.

Before the pin strokes and the falling out of bed and the calling of George next door to help him up, before what probably was Alzheimer's when most had not learned the word and "addled" was the usual description, before "E's" Parkinson's disease, Bob was involved in a patriotic way during World War II. He and "E" had sold the iron ornamental fence in front of their home on 1841 South Main Street. They'd been very proud of that fence when they bought the house and it hadn't been easy seeing the fence carted down to Old Isaac, the town's junk master, in the hopes that its melted ornamentation might help the boys fighting over there.

Bob's other contribution to winning the war was his saving of tinfoil for the aluminum that was in it. He never let a stick of chewing gum go by that he didn't peel away the wrapper's tinfoil backing, never let an empty cigarette pack escape without first removing the tinfoil covering. Each tiny square of the tin-lead alloy was then added to Bob's globe, growing in almost perfect symmetry, larger and larger until it threatened to become a bowling ball.

"Here," Bob would say to Old Isaac after walking another globe down to the junkyard mainly filled with dank-smelling tires and batteries. There weren't any aluminum globes there except the ones Bob carried down.

He built birdhouses, too, and he worked with leather. He collected antique tools and displayed them on a large board, which "E" barely tolerated above the oversized chest of drawers in the back eating room. She could hardly have denied him that much space because in the same room, she raised canaries, kept a mean parrot named "Bobby" in a cage, found room for her crochet stretching frame, and down the stairs in the unfinished basement raised baby chickens until they were ready to be put outside to become fryers for the table, the chicken for the dumplings on Sundays.

"E" never attended church, and she was not seen at Sunday School more than a handful of times, because she didn't feel anything but awkward there. That had been early on. The usual frumpy conversations, the frocks in summer, furs in winter were not the things with which she wished to compete or compare. So, she stayed home on Sunday as she did all the other days of the week.

Bob didn't attend regular church services either, but he hardly ever missed the "Old Men's" Sunday school class, and he usually recruited whatever foster child might be in the house at the time to appear before the nodding elders to read the scripture to them, jar them awake, sometimes to lead them in prayer, sometimes, depending on the talent, to preach to them like miniature Billy Sundays.

Bob and "E," either she barren or he lacking the force to create new generations, were like second father and second mother to many who spent their nights in the trundle bed on the floor of the bedroom closet. It was the best of arrangements, for it seemed as secure as a womb, certainly no problem about falling out of bed.

The Ewalt boy next door, whose name was Bobby, was thought to have been the originator of the name of "E," the abbreviated name for the straight-as-a-ramrod woman before the onslaught of Parkinson's disease, she who drew the line at whooping cough and forbade any of her foster children to cross over and play with Bobby or any other kid who'd come down with such horrifying hacking. The children stood on their respective sides and talked from an acceptable distance, each knowing it did not bode well for any kid to disobey "E." Bob was not consulted one way or the other, and he never offered an opinion, much less a directive.

It must've been near the end of middle age that Bob suggested to "E" that they care for a ten-acre farm on the edge of town, a place where he might grow a patch of tobacco, raise a few sheep and a calf or two as a source of manure for "E's" roses in town. It was the last consideration that won her over, and she agreed to the acquisition of the land that after their deaths would be surrounded by shining suburban homes, although they had not looked upon the land as a realtor would because they just didn't think that way. They thought simply about growing a good crop of tobacco that would give them pin money from the warehouse and a homemade chew for Bob when he craved it, a few good lambs that would pay for their feed, some baby beeves that would justify their keeping, a small flock of hens and a noisy Rhode Island Red rooster, and that was about it.

"Rrrrobbbb, I'll be needing manure for my roses."

To which Bob would respond only with a glance of his eyes, meaning, "I certainly will get it without fail."

Bob came dragging home a Model T truck one day, and with that he chug-chugged and oog-a-ooged from town to the farm and back again whenever "E" needed more manure for her roses. Actually, their relationship was that she was not nearly so much his as he was hers, although the way she talked about him even to his face would make a donkey wonder why she bothered at all, or why he put up with it. It would be hard to say how they really felt about each other. "Love" was never a word that passed between them whenever anyone was around and it was a safe bet as they grew older together, "love," a word that surely had been uttered at some point long ago in youthful passion, had come at last to mean companionship and security, although those words were not uttered aloud either.

Bob turned on the Crosley radio each afternoon at 5:30, Monday through Friday. He would not want to miss Amos and Andy, followed by Lum and Abner, then Lowell Thomas, Bob's only concessions to outside influence. "E" usually sat close by, pretending not to listen. She thought Bob and Abner had a great deal in common, and she held Lum to be a father figure. As for Amos and Andy, Amos was the only one of the four who made regular sense, and his natural wisdom was much admired, openly by Bob, secretly by "E."

Lowell Thomas, on the other hand, was the kind and friendly dispenser of information about that strange and desperate world outside 1841 South Main Street. If Lowell Thomas said it was so, you could bank on it, it was so. If Lowell Thomas thought it was funny, it was funny. If he thought it was serious, you'd better listen, because it was serious. Whatever Lowell Thomas said, it was right. And when he said, "Sooo long until tomorrow," there'd be a nodding all around, Bob to spit in the green-bottomed spittoon, "E" to do a final whipstitch before heading out to the kitchen to take the fixings from the stove.

It was the marbles for which Bob would be remembered most by his foster children. Bob had an uncanny ability to find marbles alongside the Clintonville Road, whenever he and a child in his keeping walked from town to the farm, the days when "E" didn't need manure and was content to water her African violets and clean out the tropical fish tank, and besides, the Model T truck was more huffing and puffing trouble than it was worth when there was no order for manure.

"There's one," said Bob, spotting another marble alongside the road.

The child hurried to pick it up, and every day they found marbles together, returning home to take down the big jar in the corner cupboard in the back room, unscrewing the lid and adding the new marbles to those found yesterday and the day before, the jar fast filling up yet never overflowing.

Years later, the farm had been sold to developers and Bob had died and Catherine had come from California to take care of "Sister," fixing it so "E" could sleep on a cot in the dining room, which was never used as a dining room but as a place for caskets for members of the family when those times came. The body of sweet, beautiful Agnes, Catherine's 19-year-old daughter, who had been thrown from the rumble seat of a car and killed in California, lay in a coffin in this room, and it was a sadness almost too heavy to bear.

After sleeping on the cot in lonely desperation, without Bob to sting with words, "E" passed away too, and so did Catherine, and they are all buried in the family plot, Bob and "E" side by side on the cemetery knoll less than a quarter of a mile from the house that had been their home in Paris, Kentucky.

In time, one of the foster children grown to manhood recalled the marbles stretching as far as the eye could see on the Clintonville Road—and suddenly, the riddle of the never-overflowing marble jar made sense. Before each walk to the farm, Bob had sneaked marbles from the jar, and he had filled his pockets. As he walked, he silently had dropped the marbles behind him—salting the roadway as he went, setting the stage for discoveries on the way back home.

Mother's Day

God could not be everywhere,
and therefore he made mothers.

– Jewish Proverb –

*I*t was a rainy day in early spring. A nice man held a large umbrella over my head as I walked from my car to the front door of the place where she lay in rest. Pauline, the mother of a colleague, had not known me personally but she symbolized that which is celebrated each year on Mother's Day—patience...love... ...loyalty...love...forgiveness...love...and God.

Grandsons helped bear the burden through the rain in Bellevue Cemetery in Danville, Kentucky, where the ground was soft to the touch of feet, giving way to the weight of the sadness of the living.

I thought to myself, "How long has it been since you placed flowers at the grave of your own mother? And will you remember to do it this Mother's Day?"

Do you remember which flowers she loved the best? Which words would she have most appreciated to be left with her favorite petals, where the water and tears wash down, causing the message to blur past recognition? Would she have wanted her son to say to the daughters and sons of mothers still living, "Go visit, go hold the hand that bathed you, fed you, helped you up when you had fallen?"

Yes, she would have wished for that.

A single institutionalized Mother's Day message is a creation benefitting the shareholders of greeting card companies and, to a certain extent, befitting the person for whom the honor is due. But to remember mothers in a special way but once a year is as impoverished as remembering a single sunrise. The card and its message, each manufactured from afar, seems precious little substitution for "being there." In the garden. In the kitchen. In the basement for the rolling of dough and the baking of bread and the making of sausage. In the washroom with sleeves rolled up past every soiled condition. In the bedroom where rest comes last to the one who has toiled the hardest, has loved the deepest, has suffered all male indignities. In the hospital for yet another birthing by herself, her daughters, her granddaughters, a common pain shared through repeated generations.

"There'd be no babies if men had to have them," Lucile used to say with a mixture of bittersweet memories. She was right, of course. *Sons Come and Go, Mothers Hang in Forever* is a William Saroyan book on the shelf next to the fireplace in the parlor of my manhood. Across the way, looking down from the opposite mantlepiece in the bedroom is the picture of my mother, Lucile, when she was only 16, three years before Jane, her first-born.

As the rain fell in Bellevue Cemetery I spoke with myself, or was it Lucile speaking with her son? "It would be nice, yes it would be very nice if you would remember me this Mother's Day with some flowers for my grave in the North Middletown Cemetery. And yes, should you want to write a little something on the card, go ahead and do that. I won't be able to know what you have written, and that will be the most important thing about what you have done. The kind of flowers I should like for you to bring? Well, yes, I did always like a single orchid, but if you are unable to afford it just now, I will be pleased with some peonies. Yes, a small handful of peonies will be quite nice.

"Do you suppose you might take from my bouquet a flower, even a single petal, and place it on the grave of *my* mother, where she sleeps just on the other side of Father? I always wanted to be next to him, as you probably knew without me speaking about it in this way at this time.

"Actually, Lala, your grandmother, would like just a pinch of baby's breath. And never mind that she would say, 'Pshaw,' and click her tongue off the roof of her mouth. Deep down she would greatly appreciate the attention. She did like you quite a bit, you know, except the time you became so angry with her when she threw that panful of dishwater on your dog. After all, Dusty had not been so very nice, and he probably deserved everything she gave him and benefitted from it too."

Was I talking with myself or was it Lucile actually speaking? The Reverend Tim said of Pauline, "She is not here...there is another life entirely apart from this." Was this peace at the center? Was this the community of ancestral mothers whispering? Yes, it was they who spoke through rain in Danville, causing me to remember Lala's mother, Catherine, who sleeps over the knoll. And Nellie, who lies in eternity by the side of Coleman, who preached many funerals in this cemetery and now rests from his labors. And Cynthia, whose resting place is lost in time.

PART THREE

The Yellow
Brick Road

Hi-Ho Silver, Awaaaay!

"To love playthings well as a child, to lead
an adventurous and honourable youth, and to
settle when the time arrives, into a green and
smiling age, is to be a good artist in life
and deserve well of yourself and your neighbor."

— Robert Louis Stevenson —

*W*hen I was a little boy about 10 years old, I counted my wealth by the number of dimes I'd saved in a small tin cylinder. It was a kind of piggy bank that held $5 when full. There was a screw in the top of the cylinder and a removable cap on the bottom. I discovered very quickly that it wasn't necessary to fill the tube to the top before a withdrawal could be made. Turn the screw, the dimes move down, the cap comes off and bingo! It's Saturday afternoon at the Schine Theater at 8th and Main. One thin dime, one-tenth of a dollar, would buy a double feature, a newsreel, a cartoon, and the latest installment in the current cliff-hanging serial.

That was 50 years ago.

Back then, if one were extravagant one could invest a nickel in a small box of Milk Duds. There might be buttered popcorn and a soft drink concoction, but that was getting into serious money. There could be a magical Saturday afternoon for about a quarter, or "two bits" as the older and more worldly-wise called it. One full-length movie might be a mystery thriller, such as

a Charlie Chan episode, and the other would be cowboys and Indians, cowboys and bandits, or cowboys and robber barons. Gene, Roy, the Lone Ranger, Hopalong, and Red Rider would have us on the edges of our seats. Although the theater managers frowned on it, some of us brought our own play guns with full loads of caps, and we managed to squeeze off a round or two to help our good buddy, Red Rider: he was my favorite because he didn't smile much and I liked that. I also enjoyed the sulphuric, metallic smell of the miniature explosives of the cap strip, something uncertain, potentially dangerous, and, therefore, exhilarating about it.

The Lone Ranger was a little too slick, Tonto was everybody's favorite and he could do no wrong, Roy was a little too pretty, Trigger was everybody's favorite, and if you really wanted to talk pretty, Trigger could have carried Roy's part in a heartbeat. Hopalong was a little too fancy, Gabby was a lot more fun and believable, but Gene was a little too silly what with him breaking into a song about the time he needed to be worrying more about the bad guys—even "Frog," his sidekick, had better sense than that. Red Rider pulled it all together. He was as handsome as Clint Eastwood who would inherit the stern-faced chores later. Bill Elliott filled Red Rider's boots better than anybody, and he was about as cool under fire as any mortal man could ever expect to be. He was Shane before there was Shane.

We playmates in '39 did not completely comprehend the weekly newsreel:

Hitler was drafting a generation of German youth; troops from Holland were sent to the German border; the Dutch liner, Simon Bolivar, was sunk by a mine in the Atlantic, 140 lives lost; Hungary quit the League of Nations; Italy invaded Albania; a half-million people lined the streets of New York City while more than 20,000 paraded in a "stop Hitler" protest. The storm clouds building in Europe would not deter the opening of the World's Fair in New York, but "The World of Tomorrow" was darkened by the unrelenting developments that would send the globe crashing into the madness of World War II.

The dimes from the little tin cylinder would now be spent on propaganda movies. John Wayne became the new Red Rider for all that was gone crazy on planet Earth. Cowboys and Indians took a back seat to a more sobering thought: even a 10-year-old boy might have to fight for his country in, say, another eight years. The German blitzkrieg greeted the decade of the 1940s. Holland and Belgium surrendered. Dunkirk became a new word for defeat. German troops marched through Paris, France. Pearl Harbor. The Nazis' Final Solution. The Philippines. The Death March on Bataan. Midway. Guadalcanal. Stalingrad. Warsaw. London. Normandy. Glenn Miller. Yalta. Anne Frank. Hiroshima. Nagasaki. It was all before the Korean Conflict, the Viet Nam War, the Persian Gulf War, Bosnia, and Rwanda.

The fantasies of a small country boy in Kentucky had turned to monstrous nightmares. He feared death greatly. He agonized about whether it would be better to be killed by a Japanese or a German. Because of all the propaganda movies, he reasoned that it would be better to be killed by a German, because it would be cleaner. The Japanese were too crazy with swords, and decapitations were hugely unthinkable. A nice, clean German tank would be better, and somehow death in that way would be more noble. Finally, the great war ended, and the survivors headed home, but the world would never be the same. Something "innocent" was gone, although no true innocence had been there in the first place. It had only seemed so.

The Black man who lived across the way in the rickety cabin came home and he seemed sad and disoriented, even though he had been a first class petty officer in the Navy.

"Was it that you didn't have a commission?"

"I only wish I had been White," he said, as he turned to walk inside the shanty that everybody knew and accepted as belonging to "colored folks."

At the movie theater, the "Colored Only" balcony seemed disquietingly noisier. Was something going on up there that we Whites hadn't noticed before? Why can't they be quiet so we can enjoy these movies? Why shouldn't they think Steppen Fetchet was funny? Why shouldn't they think Buckwheat was funny? Why shouldn't they think Mammy in "Gone With the Wind" was a wonderful and correct character? Why shouldn't they think Prissy (played so deliciously by Butterfly McQueen) was a delightful soul? Weren't Amos and Andy the best of folks—as long as they stayed in their places? Didn't Rochester and Mr. Benny have the best of relationships, as long as Rochester didn't have any White girlfriends?

"Would you want one to marry your sister?"

"Give 'em an inch, they'll take a mile!"

"Separate but equal is the law of the land."

"Race mixin' is Communistic."

"Anybody who thinks blacks ought to be going to school with whites should be taken out and *hung*."

The sit-downs and the sit-ins and the boycotts were incubating in Kentucky, and soon the news from Montgomery, Alabama, was as undeniable as it was appalling to many of my contemporaries, while I found the power and the beauty of the voice of Martin Luther King Jr. strangely exciting and naturally inevitable.

There were no more dimes in the little tin cylinder. All had been spent. There were no more marbles to be found on the Clintonville Road. They had all been played in games of "keeps," snatched up by tough little boys with hard, popping knuckles, taking all the shining bright colors, trading them for puffs of smoke and swallows of beer on midnight roads, where tough little girls played puzzling, exciting games.

In time, the movie house would be torn down, would not be replaced, and the spot where it stood would become a parking lot for cars, and it would not matter what was the color of the person behind the steering wheel.

The civil rights movement had begun, and the women's rights movement would follow, and the sexual revolution was around the corner, and the words of "My Old Kentucky Home" would be re-written, and "Dixie" would cease to be sung, and there could be no peace at the center until all these things had been exorcised, not until a cultural revolution had been fully engaged.

"What do you think you would like to study in college?" asked the middle-aged woman, the mother of Barbara, my childhood sweetheart in the summer of 1948.

"Journalism."

"Journalism?"

"Yes. I think I would like to write."

1968

"I have a dream..."

– Martin Luther King Jr. –

*I*t was not a very good year. It was the year Helen Keller died in her sleep. It was the year Martin Luther King Jr. was assassinated. It was the year Robert F. Kennedy was assassinated. It was the year of the Tet offensive, the year the United States sent 10,500 more combat troops to fight in Viet Nam, the year a record 1,100 U.S. servicemen were killed in Viet Nam in one two-week period, and it was the year of the riots at the National Democratic convention in Chicago. It was the year Soviet tanks moved into Czechoslovakia. It was the year Edna Ferber, Upton Sinclair, and John Steinbeck died. It was before anybody had walked on the moon. It was before a peanut farmer from the Redneck South had become President of the United States.

I had been assigned to the presidential campaign of Eugene McCarthy. I was Number Two behind David Schumacher and, for a while, it was magic carpet stuff: Don Quixote and the flower children from New Hampshire to Oregon, an ever-loving blast—riding high on a 727, getting by on lobster tail and chateaubriand, until that hot afternoon in San Francisco, and the boys were piling onto the bus:

"King's been shot."

"Where?"

"Memphis."

"Is he dead, for Christ's sake?"

"Don't know, don't know, don't know."

Parts of Washington, D.C., burned, and we were not riding so high anymore, but we did not know how much farther we were destined to fall.

Los Angeles. The Ambassador Hotel. Music. Crowds. Booze. VICTORY.

"It's on to Chicago!"

"Bobby has won it!"

At the Beverly Hilton, where Quixote was staying, I was on my way to my room to freshen up. I stepped off the elevator and heard:

"It was some kind of a shot."

"Who?"

"Bobby."

"What?"

"Yeah."

"May have been in the leg."

"What?"

I ran to my room. To the telephone.

"Go to Good Samaritan Hospital as fast as you can."

Later, "Go to Los Angeles International to meet Jackie coming in."

Then: "Senator Robert F. Kennedy died..."

When the funeral cortege passed the Justice Department on Constitution Avenue, there was a heavy silence. There were no words from the reporter there, for none was wanted or needed. Soon, it would be time to return to what was left of the presidential campaign. I would not follow Quixote and the flower children any farther. It was time to become Number Two behind Nelson Benton on the George C. Wallace Toonerville Trolley.

Lord, how it rained that first night in Columbia, Maryland. Nelson was not there, so I was Number One. It was not a bad feeling. Fact is, I was the *only* boy on the bus. And on the ride to the airport in Baltimore, I hunkered down while the Taylor sisters, Mona and Lisa, and "mommer'n'nem," (translated from the Wallace Southern as "Mother and Them," having its roots in a Wallace political rally: "Where's your daddy?" "He's home with mommer'n'nem.") Yes, we sang, "All I Want's a Bowl of Butter Beans," and "Just a Closer Walk with Thee."

Lord, why hast thou forsaken me? Where is Quixote? Where're

the lobster tails and chateaubriand? Where have all the flower children gone? Where *is* peace at the center? Will this movie never end? This *is* a movie isn't it? There were no answers. It just kept raining, and the bus finally pulled up to an old American Flyers Lockheed Electra—didn't they used to crash a lot? I climbed aboard, took a seat in the back (he who is last shall have a clearer view of everybody else trying to be first), buckled myself in, and prepared to go riding in and among the clouds for the first time with George Corley Wallace. I stared at him as he boarded, raincoat pulled up around his neck.

Damn, he looks so short, and look at the size of that cigar!

Hellfire, ain't no stewardesses on this plane.

Ain't no booze on this plane?

And there sure ain't no lobster tail and chateaubriand on this plane.

"Hi."

"Hi."

"Want some crackerjacks?"

"Thank you."

Opening up the box of crackerjacks: I do not believe this. I do not believe this. This is the most pitiful thing I've ever seen in my whole life. Schumacher's getting served champagne by all those pretty stewardesses and eating lobster tail and chateaubriand, and here I got myself the teenage son of an Alabama state trooper handing out boxes of crackerjacks and warm sody pop. Somepin wrong. Somepin bad wrong.

Soon as they loaded the Governor's 500-pound bullet-proof lectern on board, the plane finally lifted off the ground, shooting water to hell and gone like an airboat through the Okefenokee Swamp or the Atchafalaya River. In a storm, a rip-snorting storm, we were on our way to Boston, the home of the bean and the cod, where the Lowells talk to the Cabots, and the Cabots talk only to God.

There was thunder and there was lightning.

When he's flying, George C. is white-knuckled on the prettiest day of the year. In a storm he's a man beset by demons. While I assumed the fetal position in the rear of the plane—a lost soul amid George C. Wallace bumper stickers, George C. Wallace red, white, and blue neckties, George C. Wallace cuff links, George C. Wallace imitation straw hats, George C. Wallace for President buttons, and the 500-pound bullct proof lectern—George C. Wallace himself was up front, in the cockpit, playing navigator and God's co-pilot, like it was World War II or some kind of thing.

"Better go 'round them there."

We were dodging thunderheads like a pinball heading for the out hole. Deciding sleep was the only honorable thing to do, I drifted into a semi-comatose state along the leading edge of a front of nightmares with only Mona and Lisa's "Just a Closer Walk with Thee" to soothe my troubled spirit. In fact, I wanted to be home with "Mommer'n'nem."

"Hello, Ground?"

"Baltimore Ground."

"Come in, Baltimore."

Baltimore? What the heck's going on here? We left Baltimore 30 minutes ago, I said to myself as I woke up with a start and saw a secret service agent with his walkie-talkie sandwiched between his face and one of the rear windows.

What is he *doing*?

Navigator Wallace had given the order:

"Forget Boston, return to Baltimore."

"Hello, Baltimore, come in Baltimore."

The plane's radio was out. This is *crazy*.

We came in on a wing, a prayer, a walkie talkie, only three of four engines, and sweet memories of Mona and Lisa Taylor's "Just a Closer Walk with Thee." We spent the first night in Baltimore, home of another miserable damn yankee, that Mencken feller, who used to go around making foolish statements about us Southerners, like:

"It is indeed amazing to contemplate so vast a vacuity. The picture gives me the creeps. There are single acres in Europe that house more first-rate men than all the states south of the Potomac."

Where did he come off talking like that? Who did he think he *was*? H.L.? Shoot, give me men like H.L. *Hunt*, now there was a great American. He made his fortune pumping oil, not sitting at a typewriter and poking fun at everybody else's expense.

Feeling the need one day to be stroked, after I had been granted my request for reassignment from the CBS Washington Bureau to the Southern Bureau in Atlanta, I went out to Emory University's English Department and talked with a Faulkner scholar, Dr. Floyd Watkins. I asked him if H.L. Mencken possibly knew what he was talking about. Or, had he vastly overstated the case to make a feeble and possibly fashionable point?

"Mencken was an urbanite and he didn't know the difference between cultures. It is not that the South was without a culture. It had a folk culture and it had its flaws, terrible flaws. But it had a culture, and Mencken was too blind to see it."

It was just as I expected, and in time I came to know George C. Wallace real well, in no small part by developing a taste for crackerjacks, hamburgers with plenty of catsup on them, and learning not to miss champagne so much. To the best of my ability, I reported on George C. fairly and accurately. To his credit, he never asked for anything more than that. I figured it this way: I didn't expect George C. to be somebody he's not, anymore than anybody should have expected Billy C. to act like Jimmy C., or the other way around. The same Billy Carter who flunked English three times at Emory (he claimed four times) was, in the words of Dr. Watkins in that same English Department, "The most authentic and certainly the most visible folk figure we have in the South today."

"I think Billy Carter may be the greatest political phenomenon we've had in this country since Harry Truman. He has a completely natural and, in my mind, completely honest American character, absolutely unchanged by high office. He's very likely to be misread.

He's a joke. He wants to be a joke. That's his life. But that says nothing in the world about his integrity, the way he raises his children, his honesty in dealing with other peanut farmers. He has a heck of a lot of fun out of being an Extreme Southerner. We may be too damned sophisticated to understand somebody who can do the folk things that Billy Carter can."

Of course, this explains why Billy peed in public at the Atlanta Airport, why he jumped on the Billy Beer bandwagon, and it wasn't long before he'd told Jewish people who disagreed with him concerning his Libyan connections that they could kiss his ass. All this reinforced his role as an Extreme Southerner. Following his demise, Billy either sprouted wings and is flying around in Heaven or ended up gun-running cool drinking water in Hell, take your pick. As far as I know, the professor at Emory University returned to William Faulkner.

By the time we arrived in St. Louis, the day before the general election in 1968, I was feeling downright confident, maybe even a little cocky about the job I was doing. I was understanding the Southern Mind. That was up until I received a telephone call at the St. Louis Airport. CBS News in New York was on the line.

"We want you to go to Minnesota."

"Minnesota?"

"Yeah, Minnesota."

"Wallace isn't going to Minnesota, he's going to Montgomery, Alabama."

"That's right, he's going to Montgomery, Alabama, and *you're* going to Minnesota."

"Why?"

"You're going to be our man at Waverly. We want you to be at Hubert Humphrey's house."

"You mean, I'm not going to be at Montgomery on election night?"

"That's right."

"Well, who is?"

"Charles Kuralt."

"Charles *Kuralt*?"

"Yeah, Nelson's going to be there too, to help him. You're going to Waverly, Minnesota."

"O.K.," I said and hung up.

"Goodbye, Governor. They're sending me to Waverly. I'll see you around."

It was very cold in Minnesota. I bought a $5 pair of long underwear and a $12 pair of brogans, and I was Number One at Waverly. I stood outside in the deep, cold snow, all by myself and waited for Walter Cronkite to say, "David."

He never did.

A Speech in May, 1976

Presented to Georgia Association of Newscasters
University of Georgia, Athens

"The difference of race is one of the reasons
why I fear war may always exist; because race
implies superiority, and superiority leads to predominance."
– Benjamin Disraeli –

*A*s George Wallace would say, I've come here to shed some light. And, as the governor would be quick to add: "It reminds me of a joke. What this campaign needs is some more light shed on the issues. Reminds me when I was a boy about eight years of age, we used to belong to a little church in south Alabama. That was back before electricity came to the rural south, and one Sunday after the regular services, the minister said there'd be a business meeting later and anybody who wanted to stay for it, could—and I being curious, of course, I decided to stay. And the minister made the surprising announcement: 'I have decided to buy a chandelier—does anybody have anything they want to say about it?' And this old fella sitting next to me on the first row, he must've been about 85 years of age, and me being just eight would put him back about the time of the War Between the States (you know up north they call it the Civil War, but down here we call it the War Between the States), and the old fella said, 'yes', he had something to say about it.

"'In the first place, Preacher, we don't have the money. In the second place, there's nobody in *this*

85

church knows how to play a chandelier. And in the third place, Preacher, what this church needs is some more *light.*'"

Everybody's campaign needs more light shed upon it. But, in Wallace's case, most of the time, the light that has been turned on, especially the lights of the television cameras, have been reflected pathetically and sadly in the spokes of his wheelchair. I'd like to talk to you about that, about the wheelchair, and the effect it has had on the Wallace campaign. I use the past tense purposefully, because even though the Governor has not given up officially, even though he says he will campaign in the remaining primaries—Michigan, Maryland, Kentucky, Tennessee, Arkansas, California—just about everybody knows that the Wallace Campaign, which last year seemed to show promise, perhaps more promise than it ever had before, has turned out to be a promise with a hole in it.

You can say, as the governor does, that his achievement, his victory, has been the I-told-you-so after the McGovern debacle, the movement of the party from left to center (just how left of center or right of center I cannot say, but perhaps some of you will figure that out and, if you don't, perhaps the historians and the political scientists will come in and shed some light on it.) Perhaps it is enough for Wallace to be able to say now, as he does, I was drinking out of one well, and they (there's always a *they*, a you'd-better-watch-them-or-*they're* gonna getcha *they* in any George Wallace explanation of anything) *they* were drinking out of another well, but now *they're* drinking out of the same well. He doesn't say, "*We're* drinking out of the same well," the same dipper—*THEY'RE* drinking out of the same well.

But, I came to shed some light on the wheelchair, to shed some light on those, including myself, who put the light on the wheelchair. It was May 15, 1972, just about four years ago to the day, when the governor's legs had the life turned off in them. He had been cut down on a warm afternoon in the Laurel, Maryland, shopping center. But before the sun had gone down, there was talk among the Wallace family and staff, that Franklin Roosevelt had been elected in a wheelchair—the Governor's heart was all right, his mind was all right, he was alive, he could still campaign. As a matter of fact, he was shot on Monday, operated on Monday night, and the next day, Tuesday, George Corley Wallace had won the Michigan AND the Maryland primaries. Remember the pictures of Cornelia showing the headlines to the Governor as he lay, propped up in bed in the intensive care unit of Holy Cross Hospital?

The governor was told by his doctors that he must stop thinking about politics until his condition had improved, either stop thinking about it and start thinking exclusively about physical therapy, or forget about ever again actively campaigning. If George Wallace is anything he is a pragmatist, a politician all his life, but a practical politician who doesn't want to live *just* to live, but to live so he can keep politicking. George Wallace doesn't want to go fishing unless there's a crowd of voters there. He doesn't want to eat in restaurants unless there are voters there. He doesn't give a hoot about much of anything I can think of that does not in some way relate to politics.

George Corley Wallace was so determined to get well, he made it to the Democratic National Convention in Miami: "Larry O'Brien said I couldn't have any hotel rooms in Miami. Well, I not only got hotel rooms, I got some of the finest hotel rooms, and they even asked me to speak at the convention, and I told *them* ...."

Was it the wheelchair that was so noticeable when he spoke before the convention? or was it the sameness of the speech? or was it the miracle that he was even alive?

"I told *them*...I told *them*," the words hauntingly childlike, as if he were taunting on a playground at recess time, telling reporters at a news conference in a room off the main lobby of the Four Ambassadors in Miami, telling us—he sitting there in the wheelchair (did anybody really notice the wheelchair so much?)—but, damn it all, what would he *say*? Just a minute here, what *could* he have said that would have made a particle of difference? Of course, he would say he was on his way back to Alabama to try and get well. Of course, he didn't have time to think about anything else, but just to try and get well. Are you going to file a report on that? On what? What's there to file a report on? Give him a break, give me a break. Let's go get a damn drink. You've been following the guy too much. Where's Quixote when we need him?

George Wallace was in and out of the hospital in Birmingham, and I was there with a camera crew most of the time to record it. He was in a wheelchair, but I don't think it was so noticeable AS a wheelchair. It really came down to WHO was in the wheelchair. Did he look tired, how was he feeling, what was he thinking, would he have to come back to the hospital, could he consider running for the presidency on another third party ticket?

"Well, of course, you know I'm busy being Governor of Alabama," and no, he told the American Independent Party Convention in Louisville, told them by telephone, no, "I must get well, the doctors tell me I must get well."

So he returned to Montgomery and in 1974 he was re-elected Governor by the greatest majority in the history of the state. I did not cover that campaign. CBS would wait until '76 to see if Wallace were still around, but we knew he would be a candidate well before that. One look at the national campaign headquarters in Montgomery and you knew "Wallace in '76" was a foregone conclusion, never mind all the speculation about whether he would or he wouldn't. George C. was holding court in Alabama, and the politicians were coming to see *him*. He no longer had to go to see them, and apparently it was no longer a matter of disgrace to be seen with George C., and so Edward Kennedy came down and Richard Nixon came down, and they rolled George C. out in his shining wheelchair to see them all, yet how many then were *noticing* the wheelchair? The Wallace campaign staff was worried.

The Chinese doctor from New York made his weekly trips to Montgomery, the acupuncturist who believed he had restored "tone" to the governor's legs, had arrested the atrophy, and had said publicly he believed the governor would walk again. The governor knew better. He told the Chinese doctor not to come back anymore.

Dallas Love Field. The far end of it. Away from the gate where Lyndon Johnson took the oath of office as the 36th President of the United States aboard the plane where they had carried the shattered body of John Fitzgerald Kennedy. A decade later, a smaller plane, a Jet Commander, pulled up to a stop, the door opened and a television crew and a reporter were there with a handful of other people. One man was wearing a George C. Wallace imitation straw hat and he had a "Wallace in '76" bumper sticker stretched out between his hands (wasn't he a little early?) and Governor Wallace's press secretary, realizing there was only one television crew there said, "Look, if you won't film it, we'll carry him to the car and put him in, but if you tell me you are going to film it, it's going to take longer, and we're going to have to put him in a wheelchair and roll the wheelchair to the car and it's going to take longer." The crew could have been ordered off the ramp, there could have been a confrontation, an ugliness. The decision was decent. It was *not* to film, and so the public, with the exception of the small band of supporters, never saw George C. carried like a sack of potatoes out of the Jet Commander and put into the car. What the public did see was a cutaway of the man with the George C. Wallace imitation straw hat and the "Wallace in '76" bumper sticker and tears running down the face of that lonely man as he watched George C. carried like a sack of potatoes to that car.

About one year later, it was London's Heathrow Airport. Some far end of it. Away from the regular commercial gates. A bigger jet than the Jet Commander—a BAC 111 with "Trust the People" printed on the tail—pulled up to a stop and the door opened and many television crews and reporters were there. A few minutes before (it was pitch dark—2 a.m. or thereabouts) Governor Wallace's press secretary said to representatives of the three U.S. networks: "We can't have any lights turned on when they carry the governor down."

"Why not?"

"Because the light will be in the eyes of the security men who are carrying him. They might stumble and drop the governor."

"We're not sure we can agree to that."

"If you don't agree to it we can have you removed from this restricted area."

"Look, it's not our business to make the governor look good *or* bad."

"Sorry, but that's the way it has to be."

"Well, let me just tell you one thing, Billy Joe: we won't turn the light on if nobody else does, but next year, Billy Joe, when the campaign is officially on and it's broad daylight and we are covering the governor, we're going to film him every opportunity we can film him, because that's our responsibility and that's what we're paid to do, and you can count on it."

"That's all right, but tonight, no lights."

There were no lights when the Governor was carried down to the ramp. *After* he was in the wheelchair we interviewed him. And months later I received an inquiry from my bosses who wanted to know how come we saw Wallace at the *top* of the steps and then we didn't see him again until he was at the *bottom* of the steps? I explained, and I heard nothing more about it. But I decided then and there, that there would be no more tradeoffs. What was, *was*. What would be, would *be*.

There were endless, or so it seemed, endless articles in the press about Governor Wallace's health: his hearing; his kidneys; his bowels; his abscesses; his depression; his pain; his sex life, or the lack of one.

"How are you feeling, Governor? Are you tired?"

"Listen," he said by the time of his European trip prior to the last presidential campaign, "The only thing I'm tired about is people asking me if I'm tired. What did *you* do last night? You look kinda tired to me."

About that broken leg back in the summer of 1975:

"How did you break your leg, Governor?"

"Well, I don't know. The doctors say it probably happened during my physical therapy, but I'm all right," he said as he thumped the left leg, the lifeless leg mending in the cast. And sure enough, the leg was out of the cast in time for him to make the trip to Europe. Maybe by then many of us had forgotten about the broken leg. What did it matter? Anybody can and does break a leg. But may a presidential candidate break a leg? May a presidential candidate bump his knee on a car door and go to the hospital for it? Nixon did. But may a presidential candidate go through a campaign in a wheelchair? Roosevelt did. Four times. But, we're talking about Wallace—schoolhouse door, Clio, Alabama-George Corley Wallace. In a wheelchair?

So the "Wallace in '76" campaign began, and one of the first questions at the news conference in Montgomery:

"Governor, will you submit to an examination by an independent panel of doctors?"

"Boo. Boo." Angry looks. Nervous looks. The floor seemed to shake in the conference room of the Governor's House Motel in the Cradle of the Confederacy.

"Damn reporters. Boo. Boo."

"My health is all right," said George C. "Some of the best doctors in the country have told me that." And so, off he went to campaign in a wheelchair. Massachusetts was enthusiastic about the Governor. They came out to hear him. Filled up halls two times, two-and-a-half times on the same night, and we came to call those happenings "doubleheaders." One time there was a tripleheader; I can't remember where it was; I think it might have been Dearborn, Michigan. We learned later from his diary that Arthur Bremer was there that night too, and he had the gun with him, and he was looking to shoot Governor Wallace, but two young women moved in front of Bremer, so the shots were not fired in Dearborn, Michigan.

Nobody was talking much about the wheelchair. But the Governor's campaign headquarters staff was becoming more and more skittish about it. They put together a paid television commercial that showed George C. throwing a football. Although he looked good throwing it, the picture served only to call attention to the wheelchair. After Massachusetts, where the Governor finished third, there were misgivings about the commercial, and it was pulled out of the sequence.

On to Florida.

Beautiful, cosmopolitan, redneck, oranges-and-grapefruits, Cuban community, cattle-raising, fun-loving Florida, where—"I got 42 percent of the vote and won it in 1972."

"How well will you do there this year, Governor?"

"I can't second guess the people and I won't second guess them, but I'll do well."

That's what George C. said, but I thought I saw something else: early on, it was the very small crowd that turned out at Fort Walton Beach for a prayer-in-schools rally, and the Governor *did* look tired. Looked like something was bothering him. It was more than the rain clouds overhead. Maybe it was that he was feeling the fires flickering in the upper half of him. It was impossible for him to feel anything in the lower half of him. And later there was that strange gospel-singing barbecue, "Y'all come and BE with us and the governor at Candler, Florida." Something wasn't right. You just couldn't quite put your finger on it. It was just a little peculiar. I mean, there was the crowd spread out over a hill and one side of another hill. Thousands of people. How many thousands? I don't know, give 'em 5,000. "Shoot, had to be 15,000. Damn media."

The governor would speak from the other side of a lake. The other side of a lake? "Yep. Build you fellas in the media a special platform on *this* side of the lake."

"But, damn it, you can't hardly see him from that distance. Whose idea was this?"

"Search me. That's the way it's gonna be."

"Should've been here this morning when the frogmen checked the bottom of the lake!"

"Who in the name of creation is going to get George Wallace from the bottom of a lake? A Russian submarine?"

Finally, the motorcade wound around from the other side of the hill on the other side of the lake, the drivers parking the cars behind a high partition. At last, they rolled the Governor out onto the platform and he spoke and he spoke badly. He was so far away. And when he finished speaking, they rolled him behind the partition, loaded him into the car, and the motorcade wound back up the hill, down the road and out of sight. Had he been here? Had George C. been here? Too bad he couldn't have come over among the people the way he used to, shaking hands with the *folks*. He's gone now. He's gone. There was no light shed that day on the wheelchair, but you knew something was missing, because he looked so little. Yeah, he still talks good, but he's so little.

Pensacola Airport. "Trust the People" was parked on the ramp, waiting for the return of George C., who had been interviewed at a local television station. I was with him. He didn't seem tired today. He was feeling good. In the Panhandle. Good country. Good redneck country. Wallace country. When we returned to the plane, I stood near the wing, watching the security men carry the governor up the steps. No crews around. No other reporters. The security men and the governor disappeared inside the forward part of the BAC 111 and I sauntered up the steps in the tail. I sat down on a couch in the section just aft of the governor's private area and blended into the woodwork. The curtain was buttoned. I heard a voice, a muffled noise. At the time, it was not enough for me to react. I didn't know anything was wrong until Cornelia came back, oblivious of my presence, and she, the First Lady of Alabama, she, who would dare to dream of becoming First Lady of the United States—there *was* a physical resemblance to Jackie Kennedy, and a number of people said as much after Cornelia had flung herself on her husband as he lay in the Laurel, Maryland, shopping center parking lot after Arthur Bremer had pulled the trigger—four years later, Cornelia began talking to one of the Alabama state troopers about whether there ought to be an x-ray.

X-ray? I sat there sponging up the words.

"It was the dust cover."

"Well, he tripped and he fell."

"Maybe we can't wait until tomorrow to see a doctor."

"We could see a doctor in Panama City."

"We should call Montgomery."

Word by word, piece by piece, the details of the story came together. Before we landed, I, the only reporter on "Trust the People," had a radio script written and timed at one minute. As we taxied to the ramp in Panama City, I went forward and looked at the governor, and he looked up at me, and he said, simply and wistfully:

"They dropped me."

One of the Alabama security men had caught his heel in the floor mat, stumbled and George C. Wallace was dropped. The security man fell with some of his weight on the governor, pushing him down, causing his right leg to bend back beneath himself, straining a ligament. At the first stop, I filed the first report of what had happened:

"They dropped George Wallace today in Pensacola."

A little later, the Governor had thought better of it, and he said he was not dropped. I knew better. By this time I had a film crew. We went to the site of the evening speech. By pure luck I was walking through the lobby and overheard a Wallace supporter say, "The Governor must've stopped at McDonalds's for a hamburger."

I stopped dead in my tracks.

George C. loves hamburgers (with lots of catsup), but he never had stopped at McDonald's for one, especially when in a motorcade on the way to make a speech. That was not right. But, I asked the man where the McDonald's was. He told me the street and the address. I ran for my crew and we went tearing across town, found the street, found the address, found McDonald's and, just as I suspected, George C. was not at McDonald's.

I looked across the street. Yep. Medical Center.

I ran down one side of the rectangular building, and there was the motorcade parked in back. I wouldn't be the only reporter on the scene for long, because I went to a telephone and called the CBS Evening News with Walter Cronkite and provided copy: Wallace had been taken to a medical clinic; Wallace had been dropped; a source close to the Governor said there was a swelling of the knee; there would be x-rays in Panama City Beach. This was phoned in during the broadcast and it was public knowledge almost immediately. Other reporters began arriving. The governor's staff sent for a wheelchair that would accommodate the leg in an extended position. We filmed the arrival. An agent asked us not to. Then he thought better of it: "Oh, go ahead," he said, wearily. We had planned to anyway.

The lights were on brightly when Governor Wallace emerged with the doctor: sprained ligament, happens to professional baseball and football players all the time, it'll have to be in a cast for several weeks, no fracture. That night at the speech, they rolled in George C., his leg extended straight out...and..well...maybe it was at that point, if there had to be one moment in time, when the wheelchair became so obvious, the campaign's futility so plain for all to see. By this time, the governor had given up all pretenses: "They dropped me," he said.

That night, we did not move on to West Palm Beach as scheduled. We returned to Montgomery. George C. was stretched out on the couch in his private compartment and he looked like a ragdoll, propped up in the corner with nobody to play with him. That night he was taken to St. Margaret's Hospital in Montgomery for x-rays by his own doctor. Diagnosis in Panama City—correct; sprained ligament, no fracture. I did a standup on camera in front of St. Margaret's:

"George Wallace is vulnerable as is no other candidate in the 1976 presidential campaign." And that was the truth.

Florida was lost. And the campaign was lost.

Even George C. acknowledged, in fact boasted, that a poll by the *New York Times* and CBS and NBC indicated that two out of five voters in Florida who wanted to vote for Wallace did not because of the "health" issue, implying that had it not been for the wheelchair and Arthur Bremer's five bullets that put him there, he might have carried the South and who knows what else.

Illinois. Lost. North Carolina, maybe...maybe...just maybe...but, no. Lost. And so it went. And Cornelia insisted that the plane be turned away from the crowds so that George C. could not be seen being unloaded. Too little, too late.

George C. won Alabama, but Good Lord, shouldn't he have won Alabama? Georgia, gone to Carter. Indiana, gone to Carter. The nomination, gone to Carter.

Primary day in Alabama. The governor flew down in the little jet to Clayton and they rolled him in his wheelchair up the courthouse steps. And they took him inside to the voting booth. And they couldn't get the wheelchair in until it was turned sideways. And he couldn't pull the levers himself, so his brother, Jack, Judge Jack Wallace, went behind the curtain with him to help. And the curtain was pulled around the bulge made by the wheelchair. And all you could see, if you were there, was a crescent of spokes with two lifeless feet protruding on one side.

A woman in Pittsburgh, discovering a reporter was with one of the networks, unburdened herself: "What you and your network did was criminal...do you hear me? Just criminal...how you could have been a part of it, how anybody could have taken pictures of that man in that

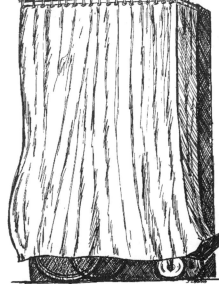

wheelchair. Some day we'll deal somehow with people like you."

A man in a crowd in North Carolina after the Governor had passed through: "I still like what he says, but you know, he seems so little."

A woman in a crowd in northern Alabama, as the Governor was speaking: "I can't see him."

"You mean you can't see *him*?"

"Nope, I can't *see* him."

A former congressman in a crowd in central Wisconsin, a reporter asking him: "How did Wallace do here four years ago?"

"He won."

"What will he do this time?"

"The other candidates are cutting into him."

"Why won't they vote for him this time?"

"The wheelchair."

"Do you blame the media for that?"

"Nope. That's the way it was."

"Well, what if the media had not reported it? What if the public had just seen him in the wheelchair when he made personal appearances?"

"It wouldn't have made any difference."

Madison, Wisconsin: a half-dozen young people were waiting for George C. in a parking lot where he'd have to be unloaded again and rolled inside for another speech, and the young people were wearing Arthur Bremer masks and they were pushing empty wheelchairs, and they were chanting, "Stand up, George, stand up, George."

It was as disgusting as it was unforgivable. The governor of Wisconsin apologized for the people of the state. Would there be a sympathy vote? There would be sympathy, but there would be no more votes.

A Speech in June, 1976

Presented to Taft Institute of Government
Trinity University, San Antonio, Texas

"The whole aim of practical politics is to keep
the populace alarmed (and hence clamorous to be
led to safety) by menacing it with an endless
series of hogoblins, all of them imaginary."

– H.L. Mencken –

*I*t certainly is a pleasure to be here with all you pointy-headed intellectuals who don't know how to park your bicycles straight. I welcome this opportunity to talk to you folks who live in ivory towers and look down your noses at those of us who might not have studied at a school of high repute—those of us who had to go out and work for a living.

As you can see, I've been following George Wallace around too long. I've lost my perspective. My judgment is warped. My opinions have hardened. My sooooouuulll is soiled, a high price to have to pay in the name of "following the candidate." Lead the candidate? No, his campaign managers *ought* to do that (some horses can't even be led to water). Get inside the candidate? Well, yes, as much as possible without being had for supper. Keep up with the candidate! That's the ticket; that's the challenge. Stay on him like white on rice. We don't have anything against RICE because of what it happens to be, we just agin big govment, always have been just agin big govment.

Stay on him without alienating him. But how do you do that? Well, how about treating him fairly for starters? Because, look at it this way: if you go up in a puff of self-righteous smoke, the candidate is going to keep on keeping on; and the assignment desk is going to trot out another reporter, jam an airline ticket up his butt, and SCREAM and SCREAM and SCREAM....

"Whataya mean you weren't rolling when he said Jimmy Carter is a liar."

"He didn't say Jimmy Carter is a liar."

"The hell he didn't, the wires say he did."

Or—"Whataya mean Wallace said Jimmy Carter is a liar?"

"I mean, that's what he said."

"Are you sure?"

"Damn right I'm sure."

"Well, you better be—the wires have not moved one word of it."

Or, in an interview in San Francisco: "Governor, did you say, 'I'll never be out-niggered again?'"

"No, I never said it."

"Did you say, 'I'll never be out-segged again?'"

"No sir, I never said it."

The problems of covering a presidential candidate are multi-varied: they are unpredictable; they are devilish; they are deceptive; they sneak up on you at night and at midday. But mainly the problems involve movement with hardly any subtleties and very little substantive thought. And maybe that's what's wrong with this country today—there is too much *MOVEMENT*: sound and fury; noise and motion; dipsy doodles; mares eatoates 'n does eatoates and little lambs eat tortillas.

Like it or not: *MOVEMENT*, physical *MOVEMENT* is the reality of interesting pictures and interesting pictures are the life blood of teleVISION. How to add substance—ah, that is the fine fiddle. The problems are complex. Some will say, well, hell no, it's simple. But most of us have come to acknowledge the elusiveness of truth. We're not against anybody because of who they happen to be, we just been agin big govment.

George Wallace is carried aboard his BAC-111 in Milwaukee or Montgomery and ABC and CBS and NBC and the *New York Times* and the *Detroit Free Press* and the *Washington Post* and *Newsweek* scamper on too, and this merry little band of mirth makers fly to Rhinelander or Nashville and the Governor is carried off and the music men follow him over to a gaggle, sometimes half a gaggle, sometimes a quarter of a gaggle: one time, only one frumpy little lady with one-dozen red roses; and the Governor says, he is just so glad to be back up here in Eau Claire and Louisville—and we not against people because of who they happen to be, we jes....

Then there's a news conference in Superior or Indianapolis and George C., "that's what they used to call me when I was a little boy: George C...." George C. puts the hay down where the goats can get it, as he did—often, syllable by syllable—as he did in 1964 and 1968 and 1972. And how come everybody still laughs at the same head recapitulator, you-tell-'im-when-he-wakes-up-that's-a-TAR-tool-and-I-got-it-at-Sears-Roebuck, I-have-decided-to-buy-a-chande*LIER*-jokes? Didn't anybody ever *hear* the damn fool things before?

And they carry George C. aboard the BAC 111 with "Trust the People" lovingly stamped on the tail, and the trombonist and the saxophonist and the xylophonist tag along and they fly to Chicago or Pittsburgh: another gaggle at the airport fence, another news conference with local reporters and the travelling press asking the same questions over and over again, and the candidate just never seeming to strike out—the pitches are too soft; the follow-throughs usually wind up being wild pitches. And it gets to be a damn boring ballgame.

What's in it for the people? Not much, really. How does he look? Looks little. Looks tired. Brave man. Damn media don't treat 'im right. Looks strong. Whataya mean, am I tired? Only thing I get tired of is people like you always askin' me, am I tired?

You and I know there ought to be more time for thoughtful discussion of the issues, but there seldom is, because the man with 97 spokes in his wheelchair has to be in Los Angeles, Phoenix, Albuquerque, Dallas, Little Rock, Baton Rouge, Mobile, Tampa, Fort Myers, and Key West, by God, and in three days too, but by now nobody's counting.

It's backbreaking. It *invariably* lacks substance. It flashes before your eyes: Was he here? Did you see him? Hell no, couldn't see him for the damn secret service and the press (the lying press deceives). This is what I'm saying: there is not enough time within the frame of reference that is part and parcel of regular television news broadcasts, not enough time to consider thoughtfully what George C. Wallace says, "We're not against people," because, for instance, on any given day, we may be grappling with such weighty matters as what did Jimmy Carter mean when he said, ETHNIC.

I have long held to the belief that too many people spend too much of their time getting too much of their news from too few sources. And, sometimes I wonder if perhaps the news-starved public won't some day heed my words of wisdom and leave me standing on some street corner in some year divisible by four, holding a microphone and saying, all alone, to empty streets, "Where did they go?"

It's true that "Face the Nation" and "Issues and Answers" and "Meet the Press" took reasonably hard runs at Wallace and the rest of the candidates—30 minutes, as if that were a long time. It is not enough time. We should know more about every candidate's thoughts, inclinations, conclusions on every issue that matters to the American people. What about morality? And if it's good enough for the goose, it ought to be good enough for the journalist. Moreover, I believe, even more importantly, the people should, somehow, have opportunities to get their views *to* the candidates; because the candidates will represent the people, and the people will decide who will fulfill the responsibilities of representation. Likewise, the people should be able to question journalists and from them, straight answers should be demanded. The playing field has serious ruts in it when journalists are unaccountable.

Regional primaries have been suggested as a possible alternative to the madness of the present 30 state sideshows. There should be more discussion of it, because it does no good to go on making fun, being cute and smug about the present system. There ought to be tough, in-depth probing of presidential candidates by the most respected reporters, by scholars, and by ordinary folks whenever possible. There ought to be fewer vaudeville acts, and a greater dedication to the idea of dialogue, give and take, exchange of ideas. The candidates ought to do some listening.

I can't predict to what extent television coverage of presidential candidates will change in the years ahead, but I have a feeling that the immediacy factor will intensify, and it will only be beneficial if it is used for something more, a lot more than simply predictable handshaking pictures. The increased compression of time, greater speed using miniaturized equipment in live hookups should make it possible to ask more questions, and not just *more* questions but more *meaningful* questions. If we could just keep the candidates from getting all spaced out: if we could establish the forums at some sensible times and places it would help immeasurably.

The challenge reaches down to this university and to every classroom in the country. Despite our newfound speed we must develop the ability to discern. We must learn more than how to move simply *in* space—as if our bodies and minds are so much expedited baggage: Delta Dash; Eastern Sprint; Braniff Pronto; Southern Lickety Split. The space encompassing our minds is infinite, if we were but inspired to know that and act upon it to improve the quality of our lives—even though we may have pointy heads and whether we park our bicycles straight or not is of less concern to us.

Let me go back now and pick up on a fragment of thought which occurred to me this morning as I stumbled out of a bed at five o'clock in Baton Rouge. An old familiar face in the mirror saying, wait a minute, remember what *Newsweek's* Joe Cummins said about the *fabric* of news, the tone of it, mood of it; the poetry, the bits and pieces of it? We in television news do this rather well, I think, if we do anything at all.

Who will ever forget some of the most memorable newsfilm, I do not hesitate to say, the finest of its kind, that has ever been rolled through a camera: George C. pumping hands on May 15, 1972, in the Laurel, Maryland, shopping center; and an arm arcs between the

Wallace faithful; and you hear five shots; and you see the smoking revolver; you see the contorted face of the youth pulling the trigger; you see George C. sprawled on the pavement (you do not see the blood splattered on the pant legs of CBS News cameraman Laurens Pierce). You see the moment of impact when a bullet strikes secret service agent Nick Zarvas in the throat. You see Cornelia throw herself on George C. to protect his head. You see Arthur Bremer wrestled to the ground. You see George C. placed into an emergency vehicle; you see it departing for Holy Cross Hospital in Silver Spring, Maryland. You do not see Laurens Pierce commandeering the Singer Sewing Machine delivery truck; you do not see him handing the driver a $50 bill with instructions to take him as fast as he possibly can to CBS News at 2020 M Street in Washington, D.C. In minutes you do see Pierce with Roger Mudd live on the set, explaining what happened to the American public.

Could we have done without all that movement? It's not relevant whether we could have or not. It happened. It was reality. And television news *showed* it with all its horror and its sadness. Of course, many of us want to do more than play cops and attempted assassins. Sometimes, because we cover presidential candidates from the time they get up in the morning until they have retired for the night, sometimes we catch our man putting both feet into his mouth; and we watch how he tries to get them out. It is most difficult to run with both feet in your mouth, even harder to run when television news cameras are on and portable and the cameraman is able to run with you.

It's earlier in 1972, before the shooting in the shopping center, and George C. has gone to make an evening appearance at a Jewish Community Center in Greater Miami. He is to speak to a group of senior citizens, but as he is walking down the hall, one of his staff says: "Governor, why don't you step into this room for a few minutes, there are some young people who want to talk to you."

George C. has always had a problem with young people not of his generation, broadly speaking. I think he always knew when he was

about to step into a lion's den filled with young, hungry lions who haven't had a Wildebeest Methodist in a long time. CBS cameraman Pat O'Dell and soundman J.W. Womack and electrician Brian Shipman (three more boys of summer) had eased into the lion's den, and all of what happened, all of what was said next was captured on film and was seen the next morning on the CBS network.

A young Jewish girl stood up. She didn't look like a lioness; maybe it was just the way she took hold of the Governor and turned him every way but loose that she so much resembled a lioness looking for fresh meat to take home to her pride:

"Governor, why did you stand in that school house door?"

"What's that, honey?"

"Why did you stand in the school house door and refuse..."

"Honey, we didn't *refuse*—we were just exercising our constitutional right."

"No, no, now wait a minute, Governor, didn't you stand in that school house door to keep *Blacks* out?"

"No, that was not it, we were never against people because of who they happen to be."

The lions roared. Some sighed. And then there was a voice from the back of the room:

"Governor, is Judaism a race or a religion?"

"What's that, honey?"

"Is Judaism a race or a religion?"

"What she say?"

Cornelia spoke directly into George C.'s right ear (whenever possible at a Wallace news conference, try to sit podium right, your left: it works better, but in any event you'll need to shout):

"She wants to know if Judaism is a race or a religion."

"Is it a race or a religion? Honey, you ask mighty tough questions...she, I, well—ah, I just happen to have with me tonight a Jewish member of the Alabama Legislature, Mike Perloff. Mike, ah, come 'ere, Mike...is it a race or a religion?"

Mike moved over, sheepishly: "I think it's a religion, Governor."

"Yeah, honey, that's what it is. It's a *religion*."

You see what happens when you have a presidential candidate, a moment in time, an aggressive television news team, and the public? You have a bit of magic, you have an insight, invaluable in helping you decide where you ought to cast your priceless vote.

I think I should like to finish with a little something that has never been said before except privately to a few friends. Perhaps it would have been the last line to a book not written on George C. for lack of a publisher and a disciplined writer.

It is Montgomery, Alabama, just after 11 o'clock in the morning, and George C. has finished a news conference at which he has formally announced that he will give his 170 convention delegates to Jimmy. The cameras have stopped rolling. It is over. Reporters are looking for telephones. Another reporter has just shaken hands with the Governor:

"Thanks for all those rides on your plane, Governor."

"That's all right, David."

A staff member smiled: "I think we charged him for all those rides, Governor."

And then, for the first time at what was left of the last news conference on the last day of a campaign that began 12 years before, George C. turned his head and said to Cornelia seated in the corner (she looked especially beautiful that morning—a deep tan, handsomely dressed):

"C'mer, honey."

She came to his side. He held up his hand and she took it as you do when you take someone's hand backwards:

"You not sorry I didn't get to be President, are you?"

"No, I'm not sorry. It didn't make any difference."

Cornelia felt deeply the bitterness of defeat. Of course, it did make a difference. It was only as much as Cornelia could think to say in an off-guarded moment. (The divorce lay down the road, around the corner, and actually it didn't make any difference to the nation whether or not it made any difference personally to Cornelia. The governor's next marriage to Lisa of "Mona and Lisa" and the divorce from her lay down the road along with the question of how much difference it made.) There was no doubt that George C., the little boy who came out of Clio, Alabama, who *did* stand in the school house door, who *did* make three presidential campaigns, *did* make a difference.

Jimmy C. owes much to George C., whether or not Jimmy C. will admit it, because it was George C. with all his warts who had the nerve, the sheer audacity to take on places like Dartmouth. It was George C. who unrelentingly in his crude redneck way roamed up and down the land for a dozen years, decrying (call it demagoguery or what you will) big government, foreign "giveaways," welfare ripoffs, crime, and the unworkableness of court-ordered busing. It was George C. Wallace who was right about the mood of the country in 1972, whatever the correctness of the mood or the morality of it— Wallace understood it.

The governor recently answered my question at a news conference in Los Angeles:

"Governor, is this the last day of your last hoorah?"

"No, this is not the last day of my Last HOOrah. The last day of my last HOOrah will proably be the last day I spend on earth."

Not long before he was shot, George Wallace had been a lion with some of his teeth still gleaming, his claws not completely bent and dulled, his roar still a reasonable facsimile of a for-the-sake-of-politics roar. George C. had cut a pretty wide swath through the Miami jungle, and he had come upon another pride of Republicans in Hialeah.

My goodness, they had loved George C., loved him like a prodigal cub. They had applauded him, pushed and shoved just to lick his face—Lord, he was their man, their hero, their king. Why, they had even been saying he could win the Florida Primary, and remember, he did win it in 1972, won it solid, whipped the biggies—McGovern, Humphrey, Muskie, Jackson, Chisholm, Lindsey—why, the Wallacites had been so cocky, one night when a protester, a supporter of John Lindsey, showed up at a Wallace rally with a chicken on a leash—George C. was supposed to be a chicken for not debating Lindsey—a Wallace staffer had walked up to the young man with that chicken on a leash and had said, "Where did you get the pig?"

Playing right into one of the oldest jokes ever fabricated: "That's not a pig, that's a chicken," the protester had replied indignantly.

"I know, I was talking to the chicken," said the Wallace man with his toothiest smile.

That night in Hialeah, George Wallace had been very much not George the Chicken. He was definitely George the Lion. He and his bodyguards had had to fight to extricate themselves from the clubhouse full of Republicans, some of them even saying aloud that he'd make a great President. Of course, a good many of them were pretty well soused, but what the hell, George C. was a SCRAPPER. And after he had finally escaped from the love-in and was safely seated in the back of his limousine, as it pulled away, he, the Kingfish, had said to me, his Jack Burden for the evening sitting next to him:

"What will I do if I win it?"

"Governor, if you are elected, you'll just have to run the country."

George C. pouted his rectangularly-shaped cave of a mouth, fitted a new cigar into its holder, lit up and puffed, presidentially.

And the car had sped along to Fort Lauderdale—past the crowded nightclubs filled with drifting snowbirds, many of them from Kentucky and Alabama, through dimly-lit intersections where fender-bender accidents could lead to race riots and media feeding frenzies beneath the palm trees invaded by killer insects.

"Where we goin'?"

"Well, Governor," said his Florida man, seated on the far side of the back seat, "there's this lady down here, been workin' real hard for you, and you jus gotta come over here and meet some of her folks."

"What kinda folks?"

"Well, Governor, all I know is, they've got this crowd waitin' for you, and they feel it's very important that you be there and talk to 'em."

His local campaign coordinator had been up against the skeptical, stubborn side of George C.

"Y'all jes keep addin' stuff on, wear me out—already nine o'clock."

And the car had sped on to Fort Lauderdale. Just before the state trooper, Meady Hilyer, had pulled into the circular driveway of a fine hotel, George C. sniffed the air for possible trouble. His instincts never sharper. The governor's press secretary, Billy Joe Camp, came from the car he was driving, and he looked into the back seat where the Kingfish and Jack Burden were waiting with the Florida contact man.

"Billy Joe, you go in there and check out that room, and you come back and tell me how it is, and I'll wait right here until you find out."

Billy Joe went inside and had been gone about five minutes, and when he came back to the car he leaned in through the window and said:

"Governor, I think it's all right. There's a few blacks in there, but I think it's all right."

Reluctantly, George C. had gotten out of the car, had entered the hotel and had walked into the large room filled with people. Suddenly he had realized all too clearly what he had suspected and feared—that he was now more Daniel than he was Lion. If he'd been Chicken he would have turned around and flown home to roost right away. But if there was one thing George C. was *not*, he was not a card-carrying Chicken. Oh, his critics would later make out a pretty convincing case that he had been known to chicken out, like the time when he crowned the Black homecoming queen at the University of Alabama, but didn't kiss her (and she wasn't too sure about wanting to kiss *him*, either). But, he had always been a fighter, golden gloves, you remember—bantamweight but not chickenweight.

The gutsy George Wallace had made his way to the rostrum despite the hoots and hollers:

"Fascist! Racist! Get 'im out of here!"

George C. had made it to the lectern and he had thrown away his unprepared script. He began telling jokes—the same old, silly, thoughtless, valueless jokes—one after the other. Told the "head recapitulator" joke. Nobody laughed. Told the "tartool" joke. Nobody laughed. Told the I-may-not-be-the-smartest-man-in-Alabama-but-I'm-the-smartest-man-on-this-here-television-program joke. Nobody laughed. He had told every joke in his book. Nobody laughed. In a deadening stupor, the crowd had just stared at George C. Finally, everybody including the Governor knew it was time for wounded animals to go home. The pride of hungry, sullen liberals had had its fill, had made its point, had had its painful fun.

Finally, when George C. had reached the safety of his car, he growled lamely to Billy Joe:

"Billy Joe, I thought you said that crowd was all right."

"It was, Governor," grinned Billy Joe, "until you came in."

Election Night

*"Politics is too serious a matter to
be left to the politicians."*

– Charles de Gaulle –

The correspondent who had covered Quixote, Wallace, and Humphrey was up the street at the Atlanta Townhouse Motel. Well, hell, *somebody* had to cover Lester Maddox. And after *he* had been mercifully put to bed, I repaired downtown to the World Congress Center to drink coffee and eat old doughnuts and nip a little Scotch, while watching Mississippi (or was it Hawaii?) put Jimmy C. into the White House, the first President from the Deep South since Andrew J., in 1865. Damn, what a night at the World Congress Center in the city Sherman burned! The crowd of thousands roared like ocean surfs, and when Jimmy C. entered the room, the noise swelled like something you had not heard for a long time, if ever—one of those primal things. And after he spoke and left the center, I stood back aways to drink in the last drops of sights and sounds of 4 a.m.

Here come Coretta King and Andrew Young, walking together, smiling...smiling...smiling...and then, they are gone. At 5 a.m., while alley cats prowled Peachtree Street downtown, you might have looked up at the world's tallest hotel and said, well I'll just be damned, I'll just be damned. They burned this city November 15, 1864, and now just look at it, and well, I'll just be damned. A Georgian is going to the White House to be President of the whole country. And an Alabamian helped him to get there. And a Kentuckian helped to report it.

Montgomery, Alabama, Cradle of the Confederacy, where only four years before on the same spot where Jefferson Davis took the oath of office as President of the Confederacy, George Wallace had boomed: "Segregation today. Segregation tomorrow. Segregation forever."

Listen to him now. Has he changed?

"We've all changed. I grew up in the days when we had segregated schools. Even the Carter family grew up in that situation. And they supported the status quo. That's all I understood. That's the way I thought it ought to be. And therefore, I stood for that system. I wasn't a hypocrite. But that system is gone and I don't want to see that system come back. So I've changed. I would not want to go back to try to re-establish the old segregated order again. I want to do what's good for all our citizens, black and white."

January 19, 1976, the day before the inauguration. Come along to the New Pickrick on Roswell Road. Another former First Lady of Georgia is scooping crushed ice into tall glasses of tea, another former Governor has finished playing Dixie on his harmonica accompanied by a Black dishwasher, who is playing the guitar.

Lester Maddox: "People ought to have the right of association and a corresponding right to disassociate. And it is my opinion that racial segregation as it was known in this country was illegal, and that racial integration by law today is just as wrong and just as illegal."

"Do you ever get tired of frying chicken?"

"No sir. The more I fry the more I like it."

"Do you have an itch to hit the road with your harmonica?"

"Not particularly, but we have an act that would go well I think in the west and in the east and maybe down round the Miami area."

"Does it make you nervous to see so many yankees coming south?"

"It makes me feel good. I don't think we have any more 'yankees.' We're happy to have them here. Some of them have complained about we got the best deal: they sent us Sherman 112 years ago, and we sent them Carter now, and they're mad, because they think we got the best deal."

The following day they inaugurated Jimmy C. but everybody couldn't go to Washington. On that day, there were three from the Southern Bureau who also appeared on the CBS Evening News with Walter Cronkite. They were very unpresidential, very uninaugural, but somebody had to mind the store. One reporter was in Plains watching a lonely, good old dog licking water from a dripping faucet. Another was in Florida, where the citrus growers were trying to save their trees. This one was in West Virginia on a natural gas story, but at one o'clock in the afternoon, I was chartering in a Cessna 310 from Beckley to Pittsburgh and helicoptering over the University of Pittsburgh campus to look straight down into what was left of Langley Hall and then taxiing downtown in time to report another explosion.

Legless Willie

"Fishing is the chance to wash one's soul with pure air.
It brings meekness and inspiration, reduces our egotism,
soothes our troubles and shames our wickedness. It is
discipline in the equality of men—for all men are equal before fish."

– Herbert Clark Hoover –

*W*illie Jones lost his legs to diabetes, but the surgeons left his knees. Willie once was a bartender at the Adolphus Hotel in Dallas, where the high flyers came in to water, some to bourbon and branch, some to sip high tea in the afternoon. The Adolphus, built in 1912 by Adolphus Busch, beer baron of St. Louis, graced Commerce Street from Field to Akard. When the city fathers negotiated with him to build it, Adolphus Busch said he wanted the best site in town and if that meant tearing down City Hall to do it, then tear down City Hall and move it someplace else to make room for what the mucky mucks had said they wanted—a first-rate hotel.

The Adolphus was beaux-arts styling, finest handicraft of artisan stone cutters, ornate sculpture, oak-paneled corridors, luxuriant guest rooms, for a time the tallest building in Dallas. There was the French Room, and there was the Century Room, where Sophie Tucker, the Dorsey Brothers, and Benny Goodman entertained. Three presidents—Franklin Roosevelt, Harry Truman, and Lyndon Johnson—slept at the Adolphus. Over the years, Charles Lindberg, Jack Dempsey, and William Jennings Bryan were among the guests. George Corley Wallace's independent party presidential campaign sort of figured it had truly arrived when the Governor of Alabama was treated like royalty in the grand ballroom of the Adolphus Hotel. Cowboy movie sidekicks were there for Wallace, and there was a lot of sly grinning going on, nervous ear-to-ear smiles denoting pleased discomfort.

When Willie bartended at the Adolphus I imagine he was always friendly, understanding and willing to listen to troubles. Willie must have listened to lots of troubles, but there had to have been many good times. Over the years I'll bet there was a passel of pretty Texas women with splendid long legs crossed, one tall and slender spike hooked to bottom rungs, anchor for the other leg to swing as much as past experience had told would be good for making the right touch. Men with their cowboy pretensions would delight in receiving so much as a brush, a faint suggestive stroke of the leg with its Neiman-Marcus mesh, a hint of "Chanel No. 5" or "Taboo."

Willie Jones understood. He wasn't dumb. He was making a living. Tips were good most of the time but especially when he "Yas-suh-ed" and "Yas-mam-ed" and "Sho-bossed" the way every reliable Texas Black man should, like he meant it to the tips of his toes back when he still had feet. Willie could be counted on to fix the drinks right, overlook the weaknesses, and celebrate the strengths in each of his customers, make the first-timer feel right at home at the Adolphus in the city where over the years Texans as diverse as Dwight Eisenhower, Sam Rayburn, John Connelly, Lady Bird Johnson, "Ma" Ferguson, Tom Landry, Ross Perot, Bunker Hunt, Billy Sol Estes, Walter Cronkite, Dan Rather, Bill Moyers, Sam Donaldson, Lee Harvey Oswald, Van Cliburn, and uncounted Miss Texases traipsed in and out of town like cattle drovers on their way to their Abilenes.

Willie Jones saw it all, felt it all, heard it all, smelled it all, but

dared touch hardly any of it, because he knew the limits of his place in the scheme of the social, political, and economic order of the time. Willie had an important career ahead of him, but he never could have predicted, never would have imagined that he would lose his legs but at the same time, gain enough peace at the center to compensate him for the terrible catastrophe.

Willie went home to fish.

About 75 years after City Hall was torn down and replaced by the Adolphus Hotel, Willie Jones arrived early most mornings on the north side of Bachman Lake at the end of the main runway at Love Field, and you could set your watch by it. He would arrive unheralded in his station wagon specially equipped for him to drive with only his hands. He always stopped in the same place, alongside a vine-covered chain link fence, and after he had opened the door he would slide out slowly and ease himself to the ground. Willie had been a big man, but after the surgery, he wore large leather pads on the stumps that once were knees connected to legs, legs connected to feet.

Willie walked on his knees to the rear of the station wagon, opened the door and took out his polished wheelchair. He opened it up and set the brake on it. Then he began taking out the things he'd need to fish—the tackle box, the minnow bucket, the cricket box, the knife for cutting line, the knife for cleaning fish, the bamboo poles, the metal casting poles, the portable radio, and the blanket he would spread out so that everything would stay neat and Willie would have a comfortable place to sit.

Willie walked on his knees, muscling his wheelchair before him like a determined gnome hauling precious coal in a wheelbarrow. Willie looked both ways before crossing the jogging path. Runners and walkers generally moved counter-clockwise, but some came clockwise around the three-mile loop. Overhead, the first flights of Southwest Airlines roared and lifted up from the main runway, the passengers heading down to Houston or out to Midland-Odessa, the tops of the cedar trees waving on the bottom of the turbulence of the

737 jets, the fumes dark and acrid, searing new growth, gnarling the crowns, the same runway that had received Air Force One on November 22, 1963, and had provided the way for the new President, Lyndon Baines Johnson, the new first lady, Lady Bird, Jackie, the former First Lady, and all that was left of Lancelot, to return that terrible day from Dallas to the nation's capitol.

Willie crossed the jogging path beneath the thundering jets, past a huffing runner.

"Morning, Willie."

"Morning," said Willie, not knowing the name of the young woman dressed in silky yellow shorts, leg tendons tight and thigh muscles glistening with beads of perspiration, the hair above the taut face tied in back, bouncing with the movements of the nimble body.

Willie stopped at the water's edge, began unloading his wheel-chair, spreading the blanket and smoothing out the edges and corners, placing the fishing implements in their accustomed places, the radio positioned near the center of the blanket where Willie could easily reach it. He was never in much of a hurry to turn it on.

Willie's first work was to cast out and hook the "rubber line" submerged near the center of the lake. Only Willie knew the approximate location of the line, hooked and baited with 12-inch spacing. He had anchored one end of the snare at a secret below-water location a short distance from the lake's edge. To the other end of the line he had tied a large rock with a strip of inner tube to allow movement without giving up mooring. It naturally attracted fish and on a good morning when Willie hauled in the line he had his catch for dinner.

Willie methodically coiled and re-baited the line, looked both ways as well as over his shoulder to be sure nobody was watching, then threw the rock to a new location in the lake.

"Good morning, Willie," shouted a man running counter-clockwise, who could have been an executive trying to complete the three-mile track in 30 minutes, shaving off a few seconds.

"Morning," shouted Willie. "You're looking good!"

Willie settled back for a morning of fishing with the bamboo poles, from time to time casting out over the "rubber line," making sure the lure returned near the surface and did not sink and tangle with the snare. By late morning, Willie would be ready to pack it in and head for home. Each piece of fishing gear would go into the wheelchair in reverse order from how it went in. Next the radio. Finally the blanket.

Willie returned to his car, pushing on his knees the wheelchair. He unloaded the wheelchair into the back of the station wagon, folded the wheelchair, and stowed it in last. Then he walked on his knees to the driver's side, where he opened the door but did not get in until he had answered a question.

"What do you think about as you sit there without legs, fishing, seeing the runners going by, some saying 'Good Morning,' some saying nothing at all?"

"I think to myself, there they are with legs and they are running, but they never seem satisfied with how well they're running. Me, I don't have any legs, and I can't run, and I'm well pleased."

"Will you be back tomorrow?"

"No, tomorrow's Sunday." Willie's eyes were watering. "If the Good Lord can give me six days to fish, then I can give him one day just for Him."

Willie Jones pulled himself up onto the driver's seat. He closed the door and drove away.

The Apology

The weak can never forgive.
Forgiveness is the attribute of the strong."
— **Mahatma Gandhi** —

*H*ad a call from a journalist down in Alabama, who said he had received a sad note from Governor George Wallace. The message was an apology. Governor Wallace wanted the reporter to know that he, the governor, was sorry for having thrown a temper fit at a news conference 27 years before.

"It was as if he were trying to clear the decks—hell, he didn't have to do that," said the reporter.

The time had come for the writing of such notes, as many of God's children had begun clearing the decks, searching for peace at the center.

"Dear David:

"Congratulations on your book, *Follow the Storm,* which I have just finished reading. From time to time I kept up with you from your reports on CBS; then I missed seeing you. Your book fills in the gaps for me and revealed a side of you that I had not known. I am glad that I have had the pleasure of knowing you as both a journalist and as a friend.

"I am glad you escaped death and serious injury. You had some real close calls and some real struggles with your soul. I am sure that you are a better person as a result. I am thankful that in all your experiences, you have realized that what is important in life is the relationship a person has with our Lord and Savior, Jesus

Christ. That is the only real peace, a peace that passeth understanding. I share your joy in knowing that you have found that
peace at the center.

Sincerely yours,
George C. Wallace."

In his 1994 book, *George Wallace, American Populist*, Stephan
Lesher has described a meeting in 1987 that would have been most
unlikely 20 years before. Jesse Jackson had made his pilgrimage to
Montgomery to visit a forgiving George Wallace. The man who had
stood in the schoolhouse door, the man who had said, "Segregation
now, segregation tomorrow, segregation forever," asked the Reverend
Jackson to pray for him.

Jackson prayed:

"May he (Wallace) share the courage of his convictions and to use
every breath to encourage people to come together, to study war no
more, to say no to violence, to fight for that bright day of justice
when all of God's children—red and yellow, brown, black, and
white—will come together and be precious in thy sight."

George Wallace and Jesse Jackson said, "Amen."

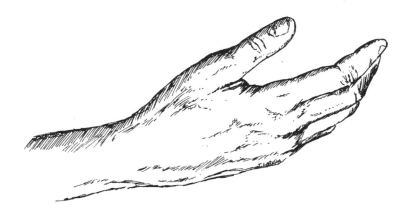

"Happy"

"You are correct in assuming that I am interested
in the welfare of every under-privileged man,
woman and child in the Commonwealth."

– Albert Benjamin "Happy" Chandler –

*T*he ancient tree in "Happy" Chandler's front yard had become
even more gnarled, but it stood as a sign of strength and
longevity. Elm Street in Versailles had changed very little over the
years. When a visitor called on a 1990 morning, "Happy" was
finishing his breakfast.

"He likes to have his breakfast alone," said Mrs. Chandler, who
greeted the visitor in the library. There was cream in her coffee and a
smile on her face.

"When I was a boy I saw a baseball game with you," said the
visitor. "We sat in the commissioner's box at Crosley Field in
Cincinnati."

"Mama" sipped her coffee, nodded that there was a possibility that
was so and waited for more information. Her son, Ben, came in and
gave his mother a hug. Ben, the publisher of *The Woodford Sun*, and
the visitor, then the publisher of *The Bourbon Times*, had been
fraternity brothers at the University of Kentucky. Ben had read the
visitor's account of how former Alabama Governor George Wallace
had been writing to acquaintances, attempting to heal old wounds.
Ben had written in his own weekly column that Wallace had written
"Happy" the past summer and had apologized to him for something
that had happened in 1968.

"Dear Happy:
"There has been something on my mind and heart for many
years. Back in 1968, when you accepted to run as the vice

president candidate with me on the third party ticket, I was very elated and happy that you would do so. However, I wanted to be sure that we were on 50 ballots because it would be the first party that ever ran that had ballot position in all 50 states. The time for electors in the states had passed, and there were at least six states' electors who were going to resign if you were on the ticket.

"When you run in a campaign of this sort, you have to take whoever you can get to run as an elector, especially in those states in which you had no chance of winning. Even the electors in your own state, whose names I don't remember, threatened to withdraw if you were the nominee. We had so many 'way off' people—way off in left field or right field—that really embarrassed me because I wanted you to be on the ticket.

"I told your biographer, who came to see me some years ago, and I sincerely hope he prints what I said. But please accept my apology even at this late date at the way in which I treated you. I had someone else to tell you. I didn't even have what it took to tell you myself. I was in your state during the time you were running for the United States Senate and when you had a large road-building program. I was selling magazines in Kentucky all the way from Hickman to Hazard and all through the Bluegrass, which is some of the most beautiful country in the world.

"I remember one time when I was catching rides home from the University of Alabama that I was on Highway 31 out of Birmingham and you and your family came by in a car. I recognized you, and on the tag was 'Kentucky 1.' I waved at you and your family, and you waved back. I told many people of that because I was very proud of it. You have been one of the most colorful characters in American political history and one of the most successful, and you did so many good things for Kentucky and for the country. Your serving as baseball commissioner was certainly a jewel in your accomplishments.

"Again, Happy, please accept my sincere apology because I wanted to get it off my mind because my mortality may yield at any moment because I have been a very sick man for the last several years as a result of the shooting that took place in Maryland in 1972."

"Happy" had called Governor Wallace on the telephone after receiving the letter, to tell him that everything was all right. The two former governors were reaching across the South, from Versailles to Montgomery, like the branches of two aged trees, as if saying, "Here's some shade."

"I don't think he heard me too well—he has that hearing problem," said "Happy" to the visitor.

"I think I want to drive down to Montgomery to see Governor Wallace," said the visitor as he prepared to depart.

The handshake of "Happy" and the visitor was warm and firm, and the ancient tree in the front yard was drawing a new ring unto itself to mark the passage of another year.

"Something has happened that was not in your morning newspaper," said the professor to the young high school students in the Minority Journalism Workshop at the University of Kentucky.

"'Happy' Chandler has died."

The radio that morning had carried the news that Albert Benjamin "Happy" Chandler had died at 3 a.m., June 15, 1991. The students looked up from the work they were doing on their workshop newspaper. No one said anything. It seemed clear no one was sure who "Happy" was.

"He's the former governor, United States Senator, and baseball commissioner. He played a major role in Jackie Robinson becoming the first Black to play baseball in the major leagues."

The awkward and total silence was an indication that the students might not even know who Jackie Robinson was either. The professor decided not to ask if that were true. Older and more experienced students in the professor's Writing for the Mass Media class were given the assignment to cover "Happy's" memorial service in Memorial Hall, a stone's throw from the journalism building.

"Your job is to report what happens—who is there, what is said, how it looks, and how it sounds. It does not matter what you think of former governor Chandler. Remember: look and listen *very* carefully. You are the eyes and ears of those who would like to attend, but cannot."

Tuesday morning, June 18, 1991, the students led the way to Memorial Hall. The professor followed. Inside, he confided to three of his students: "It's hard to describe how it feels not to be working today as a reporter. It's more satisfying to be watching you learning how to do it."

The professor saw Mimi Chandler, "Happy's" daughter, standing by the side of her father's coffin. Mimi and the professor shook hands. They had worked together briefly at WVLK in Lexington. The professor had been trying to be a disc jockey. Mimi had been trying to be a movie star. For both, the results had been mixed, at best, with the better part of the success on Mimi's side. "Mama" sat silently in a chair near the coffin. Her grandson, Ben, standing next to Mimi, seemed to be the one to whom the political torch most likely had been passed. In many ways, Ben resembled the elder Albert Benjamin in the picture standing among the floral arrangements.

Ben looked like a future governor.

"Good luck, Ben."

"Thank you."

"You know, you look a lot like that man up there in that picture."

Ben's smile was soft and deep. Maybe, at a later time, he might flash the smile that had helped earn his grandfather his nickname. Or, maybe, it would remain soft and deep. When "Happy's" recorded voice was heard one more time, singing "My Old Kentucky Home," it put a lump in the former reporter's throat. He had wondered if the recording would sound embarrassingly sentimental. It didn't. It sounded right. "Happy's" voice was strong and clear. Perhaps, no other living person would ever sing it more humbly, and at the same time, powerfully.

What the professor had not counted on was the playing of the University of Kentucky "fight song." There was no reason to believe that it would be appropriate for a memorial service. But, when Schuyler Robinson's hands touched the keys of the organ, and the carillon bells responded to his improvisation, "On, On, U. of K." never sounded with such poignancy. Nor was there any reason to believe that "Happy Days are Here Again" would be fitting for a memorial service for a former governor, or for anyone for that matter. Yet, once more the university organist improvised.

It was lovely.

The young man mowing the grass of the Pisgah Church Cemetery in Woodford County stopped long enough a few days after the private burial to point a visitor in the direction of "Happy." The visitor stood by the side of the covered mound of dirt and thought for a few moments about what Kentucky had lost.

The commonwealth had lost one of its most effective, if not finest governors. It would have to look to the future. The visitor promised himself to return in spring, to witness the Dogwood tree blooming at the head of the grave of Albert Benjamin "Happy" Chandler.

The Last Visit With George Wallace

> "The play is done; the curtain drops
> Slow falling to the prompter's bell.
> A moment yet the actor stops,
> And looks around, to say farewell."
>
> **– William Makepeace Thackeray –**

*D*ogwoods were in bloom, the petals blowing on Zelda Road, Gatsby Lane, and around the corner on Fitzgerald Street in Montgomery, Alabama, on that rainy afternoon, March 23, 1994.

Elvin Stanton was waiting where the wisteria hung in damp clumps of lavender. He held a large red and blue umbrella carefully and kindly over our heads as we walked through the iron swinging gate, past the state trooper's guard post, then into the house to the room with the hospital bed.

George Corley Wallace, four times the Governor of Alabama, five if counting the administration of his first wife, Governor Lurleen, could hardly be seen behind the unfolded, spreading newspaper, a swirl of cigar smoke drifting upward. He had just returned from another day of fundraising at Troy State University. He put the newspaper down and reached up and out to shake my hand. The grip was firm. The smile was warm yet grim.

125

There was unremitting pain without words.

It was the first time we had seen each other in 18 years. The five bullets that had cut down the governor in the prime of his life, perhaps the pinnacle of his political career in 1972, had ravaged but still not defeated all the determined, campaign battle-scarred body. Moments before the shooting, I had driven away to prepare a report for the CBS Evening News. Had I been at my accustomed spot, next to the governor's right shoulder with my arm extended in front of him to capture sound for radio, I probably would have been hit by at least one of the bullets.

Now, he was still hanging on, still surviving after 22 years of excruciating pain, his deafness total and no longer disguisable, and I wrote messages with a large, black, felt-tipped pen on ruled, white paper furnished by Elvin, the governor's press secretary who had lasted the longest. I did not ask the governor about the pain, because it was too obvious to belabor, choosing not to say I was sorry, because I knew he didn't want to hear that.

"How are George Jr.'s chances for governor?"

Wallace had recently flown to Bridgeport in northern Alabama to campaign for his son.

"Lt. Governor," he corrected me in a voice that was barely above a rasping whisper.

"Then—governor?"

George C. Wallace smiled, but his right hand still held the place where the bullets had torn up his insides. He guided my hand to his stomach, pressing my fingers down to the corset holding him together. "It feels like everything wants to push out," he said.

In Bridgeport, supporters had numbered only about 80 (members of the former governor's security staff had wondered aloud, "Where's the people?"), but George Wallace Jr., currently the State Treasurer, had told the uncommonly small crowd: "The blood in his veins runs in mine." But, in the primary, George Jr. finished third among three candidates. Later, an Alabama newsman said, "He seemed relieved."

At his home in Montgomery, the governor waited for more handwritten messages from the retired CBS News correspondent at his bedside who'd covered his three presidential campaigns.

"I have cancer of the prostate," I told him, thinking he might want to know that.

"I'm sorry," he said with eyes tired, voice weakened, the words difficult to understand.

"The prognosis is good," I told him, feeling grateful that the *only* problem I had was cancer of the prostate, wanting to be positive in some way that might give the governor reason for optimism for a friend if not for himself. We spoke of Governor Lurleen, and he asked Elvin to bring her voting record from the desk as a way of remembering her great popularity in the days before her own terminal cancer.

Wallace was pleased that Jesse Jackson had recently introduced George Jr. to Black church congregations in Birmingham, and the governor again insisted that racism had never been the issue.

"Racists hate," said Wallace. "I did not hate."

"Will you still meet with Bremer?"

The response was difficult to understand, but it seemed to be saying, "yes," if it were possible for such a meeting with Arthur Bremer, the young man who had fired the five shots into the governor that afternoon so long ago in Laurel, Maryland.

Wallace recalled the days before World War II when he traveled through Kentucky as a magazine salesman. I drew on the writing pad an outline map of the commonwealth, and together we filled in the names of some of the places he had visited as a teenager: Lexington, Paris, Winchester, Versailles, Somerset, Covington, Henderson, and Hickman.

Before leaving, I wanted to say something about Wallace's complaint that I had put him in dialect in my recent writings about him.

"No more dialect! It was hard to resist putting you in a southern accent. I did it in good spirit."

A slight smile countered the pain on the governor's face.

"Exaggerating my southern accent helped me sell magazines," he smiled. Then he added, "Yaaalll."

Lalie, our child, Ravy, and I turned for the door. "We're going to leave you in peace. Thank you, and God bless you."

As we walked back out into the rain and the scattering Dogwood petals, Governor George C. Wallace blew Ravy a kiss.

PART FOUR

Learning

Ties That Bind Students and Teachers

"The fault...lies with all of us— the politicians, the press, and the public that tolerates an educational system that turns out a population which in large numbers is too illiterate to participate meaningfully in a democracy."

— Walter Cronkite —

*T*his is the quiet time on the campuses, the window of winter and the expectation of another spring. The students have not yet arrived. At this writing, they're still extracting themselves from holiday pleasures. The well-worn paths criss-crossing the spaces among dormitories, fraternity and sorority houses, and classroom buildings are eerily still.

A sparrow chirps.

A squirrel rustles the dried and bending branches.

Some computers hum, their bytes diligently at work.

It is a time for careful consideration of the challenge lying just ahead, when the students return like purple martins to fill all the spaces now so unnaturally empty. What new thing can be told just a little differently in order to ensure a more lasting impression the next time around? How best to handle that student with a real problem of, perhaps, chronic depression, and all those needing the most compassionate help? How to motivate the obviously talented one who finds sleeping late too delicious to resist? How to challenge the excellent without discouraging the disheartened or those disadvantaged by being not so very bright? How to help the 19-year-old single mother, who in order to attend class must leave her child at a daycare center? How to encourage the young man who drives a delivery truck and who is desperately in love and who begins to accumulate many classroom learning incompatibilities?

Teachers worry about these things more than many might suppose. Most of us really want to be good, which is to say, we desire to be effective and for no other reason than we believe the students deserve it. "He who can, does. He who cannot, teaches," said George Bernard Shaw. Of course, there's just enough truth in this old saying to make it sound profound as well as entertaining. It's probably more correct to say, "He who can, does, *then* teaches," for nothing produces greater learning and better doing than the teaching of the matter, whatever it happens to be. From my own perspective, I feel as if it would have been well-nigh impossible for me to teach without my having first gone out into the world, rolled up my sleeves and gone to work.

It's a grave ingratitude to put down all teaching as if it were some fail-safe for failures. True, some wearing the title of teacher cannot do it and therefore should not be doing it at all. Some, as I, should retire at age 65 in order to become students again. Sometimes it is difficult to rid the system of these square pegs in round holes. Some were never right for it in the first place, some have grown tired over the years and some are clearly more qualified for more productive "real world" endeavors. Professionalism in education requires all its participants to be honest with themselves, then honest with the students who show up on their doorsteps. They've asked for help and in the bargain they have paid handsomely in advance. The system does not provide for money-back guarantees.

At this time of introspection, one teacher is reminding himself that he is, after all, first a student and forever a student. In fact, the students frequently become teachers and the teachers come to be their students' students. This can be a tricky arrangement, and it can lead to serious problems, but too often, the choice is to take the position that the teacher knows everything and the student knows nothing and the student is a mere glass to be filled by a water bearer whose well contains questionable sediment.

Too often, the thirst for knowledge becomes a quick gulp rather than a considered sip. Students are not alone in wanting immediate and simplified answers to most all questions, and when the Kentucky cardinal "what-cheers?" outside the window in this quiet time, it becomes a reminder that teaching is like orchestration—it takes more time, more instruments, more musicians and practice, practice, practice. Simple tunes are dandy upon a good many occasions, but the richness of chords, harmony, balance and proportion raises music to heights that truly soothe the savage breast.

"Should I leave school, because actually it's not what I really enjoy?" laments a student coming in from the cold.

"Of course, you should not stay if your heart is not in it. Go take a job somewhere, think of it for a while, and perhaps you'll return one day."

"Yes, but I might not want to come back."

"Of course, you might not, and what is so wrong about that? Many have done quite well without college degrees."

"Yes, but it will seem so incomplete without the degree."

"Perhaps, but you can't have it both ways, now can you?"

"But, I'm afraid they may not want me out there unless I have the degrees."

"That's possible. But you see, there's no fail-safe for anybody. There's no net to catch you on every occasion when you may have the misfortune of falling. So, stay in school and study. Be patient. Pace yourself. There'll be plenty of time later for all the days of your life. Remember, you are not here to be trained for a job...you are here to be educated for life."

Mr. Ben

"Man is a tool-making animal."

– Benjamin Franklin –

*T*here are those occasions that provide new and rich under-standing concerning our past, present, and future. Such was the "The Pittsburgh Conference," a gathering of professional photojournalists and graphics artists sponsored by *The Pittsburgh Press.*

What Gutenberg was to the printed word more than 500 years ago, computerized graphics are to newspapers today. Most readers take for granted this magic known as graphic art in the journalism profession. Yet, pick up almost any current piece of printed material and the work of the graphic artist as well as the photojournalist is there, clarifying, illustrating, simplifying issues and events unlike anything Gutenberg ever dared to dream.

In fact, desktop publishing has taken information availability and distribution light years beyond the time about 250 years ago, when Pittsburgh was hardly a gleam in a Chamber of Commerce eye. In the place of a sparkling, modern city at the juncture of the Allegheny and Monongahela rivers there was a simple Indian village, a culture fated for destruction at the hands of the French and the British. Colonial printers such as Benjamin Franklin and his brother, James, had labored long in their primitive shops in Eastern Pennsylvania to produce the words that would help to win freedom for a new nation. How old Ben and his Poor Richard would have marveled if they could have attended "The Pittsburgh Conference."

"MacWrite," "MacDraw," "MacPaint," and "Windows" would have dazzled Mr. Ben beyond all telling. Yet one wonders if the ghost of the old printer's devil would not have placed a gnarled finger to the side of his nose and mused, "It's technologically astounding, true, but what do you intend to *do* with it? How do you plan to use it? And will you expect institutions of higher learning to minimize the study of European history and literature in order to train technical operators for your bottom-line corporations?"

"Well, Mr. Ben, most of us attending the Pittsburgh Conference are aware that what we have available to us is nothing more than a tool, a highly sophisticated tool to be sure, but still a tool as basic as smoke signals, surveyors' quadrants, ships' sextants, and, later, steamboat whistles."

"Go on, young man, I'm listening," said the spirit of Mr. Ben as he looked in awe at the skyscrapers, the bridges, and the brilliant lights leading to the juncture of the two rivers, which form and send on its way the beautiful Ohio River.

"Where is this taking us?" he asked.

"It is not so easy a question you pose, sir, but I'll try. You see, it appears we journalists today believe there is no such thing as too much information. Having said that, many of us also believe we need all the help we can get to make sense of the information explosion. It is just as easy, maybe easier to distort—if you'll pardon me for saying so, sir—with a few pithy words such as your Poor Richard might utter, as it is with volumes upon volumes of words and megabytes in our modern information systems."

"I'll grant you that much, so—go on, go on."

"What we need here at the headwaters of the Ohio is a new commitment to truth-seeking and truth-telling. As you know, I'm sure, the first newspaper in Colonial America, *Publick Occurrences, Both Foreign and Domestick*, lasted only one issue because public officials found truth-seeking and truth-telling to be detrimental to the status quo. And then, the *Boston News-Letter*, the first *continuing* newspaper in the colonies, existed because it allowed itself to be *'published by authority.'*

"I became well aware of that problem, and brother James and I resisted it with all the strength we could muster, but tell me more about—what do you call it—desktop publishing? Is it affordable? A penny saved, you know."

"It really doesn't matter whether we can afford it or not. It is here. It is here as surely as that Indian village and its culture were wiped out at the meeting of the Allegheny and the Monongahela. It's here as surely as you drove out the British and formed a new nation with a new Constitution and a First Amendment that included freedom of the press. It's here as surely as man landed on the moon and there are communications satellites parked in what your generation, sir, called the 'heavens.'

"Let me just speak as one Kentuckian to one Pennsylvanian. You have given us our Ohio River, which on this occasion symbolizes a new stream of knowledge, a new wave of communications technology. For our part—from the Big Sandy to the Cumberland and the Tennessee Rivers—we want to add our experience, our hopes, and dreams for the future. We no longer desire isolation, nor will we rationalize, much less tolerate, complacency or backwardness of any sort.

"We have no reason to enter the 21st century with anything less than the best informed, which is to say, the best educated people in the liberal arts."

I looked all around, but he was gone.

"Oh, yes, Mr. Ben," I called into the night, "thank you for flying that kite."

Training is One Thing, Education is Another

"The man who reads nothing at all is better educated
than the man who reads nothing but newspapers."

– Thomas Jefferson –

*W*hat's good for a journalist should be good for a secretary," said
I, the journalist, to a statewide meeting of an international
organization of professional secretaries meeting in Lexington,
Kentucky.

"I wear several hats: college professor; weekly newspaper publisher; father of a child who will be 6 years old next month; shepherd;
and messenger.

"As soon as I leave here I'm going back down to the farm, because
this is sheep-shearing day. You probably know what it feels like to be
shorn."

The secretaries laughed.

"But that's no reason secretaries have to be sacrificial lambs."

The secretaries applauded.

"...or, God forbid, led off to slaughter."

The secretaries laughed somewhat nervously.

Then I turned to the meat and potatoes of my message: a word
about the "training" of secretaries, or the "training" of journalists as
opposed to the "education" of secretaries and the "education" of
journalists.

"My colleagues and I at the School of Journalism at the University
of Kentucky have an abiding belief in and commitment to liberal arts.
Most of the education of a journalist at the University of Kentucky
occurs *outside* the School of Journalism: in philosophy, history,

English, political science, economics, psychology, sociology, anthropology, theater, theology. We resist pressures from students and professionals in the field who insist that training in a vocation is to be preferred over a 'nebulous' liberal arts education. Many journalism practitioners pay lip service to liberal arts, but underneath a superficial crust of diplomatic agreement there's a quick-fix mindset: hire them as cheaply as possible, burn them up, replace them with new cannon fodder, and keep repeating the process.

"I had a small-town newspaper publisher call me aside recently and tell me what the journalism graduate should know and be able to demonstrate the first day on the job: how to sweep the floor, make the coffee, handle the phone calls, sell ads, know the way around the courthouse and city hall, take pictures, develop pictures, and lay out the newspaper. In short, make money, and ethical, sensitive thoughtfulness is left to compete with the yellow journalism of garish headlines and gruesome minutiae of tabloid detail.

"My response: we're not going to do that."

A university is not the place for teaching people how to tie their shoe strings, how to type 30 words a minute, how to know when "lie" or "lay" is correct, how to spell, how to recognize fundamental grammatical errors, how to listen to a police scanner with one ear and an irate public official with the other, how to know when it is better to write in the inverted pyramid style or to know when a perfectly normal pyramid is just fine and when no pyramid at all is quite acceptable, how to dress for the job, how to massage the publisher, and precisely when to tell the publisher, "Hell, no, I quit."

We shouldn't be "noodling the goose" at our universities. That's the method of stuffing noodles down the gullets of geese after their feet are nailed to boards, the result—liver paté. It's gourmet dining, but it doesn't say much for the goose. Learning for humans will seldom occur unless the learner arrives motivated and prepared to receive, process, and modify information.

A German scholar in the College of Communications and Information Studies at the University of Kentucky, Joachim Knuf, has confirmed this revolutionary idea that could hardly be simpler or more correct. Yet, there are those who still believe the fault for not learning resides mainly with the teacher or the educational system. Professor Knuf, educated at Oxford, believes the missing element is the one that's most essential: the learner must assume fundamental responsibility for learning. The learner must *want* to learn. The learner must come, most importantly of all, *prepared* to learn. Only then can something positive happen.

Change must occur. The learner should leave the learning environment with *changed* thinking. It does not need to be revolutionary change (although sometimes that's not a bad idea when royal folks go off thinking they're smarter than common folks). Change does not have to be monumental. It can be subtle. Students or parents who stubbornly resist changed thinking or behavior are as hopeless as the goose with its feet nailed to the board, its gullet open for all the noodles that can be shoveled into it.

The phenomenon of learning is the completion of circles. Communication that does not produce greater understanding, more refined and heightened sensitivity, and awareness of possibilities is a communication that has failed. Parents should cooperate by sending better disciplined, better motivated student-learners to the first level of formal education—the elementary school. After K-12, there *may* be a greater likelihood for advanced learning at the college level where individual responsibility, credibility, and accountability are the foundations upon which all else rests.

Truth-seeking and truth-telling in a free and open society are never neat, nor were they intended to be. In the same way, training to become what paramilitary newspaper editors envision as the most practical way to prepare for "careers" in their shops is work better left to trade schools. The mission of a liberal arts institution by its very definition should be preparing students for *life*, first—jobs, second. The student educated for a life is the human being better prepared for a wide range of "jobs." The student trained more narrowly for a job will find herself or himself more easily shoved aside in a world where rapid technological change has become a way of life and a matter of survival.

Secretaries understand survival tactics and in the speech I made to their statewide organization in Lexington, Kentucky, I discussed the problem of lying, which is commonplace throughout American society. "We're all a bunch of liars," according to H.L. Mencken, doubtless a "truth" for which we should not have to make a general apology—however, "Secretaries should not be *expected* to lie."

The secretaries applauded.

"They should resist it at all costs. We should be moving toward a *more* truthful society, because truth-seeking and truth-telling should be the work not only of journalists, but of *everybody* in society. This is the work of the messenger, and too often the messenger is confused with the message.

"Tell the person for whom you work, you are the messenger, not the message."

The secretaries applauded, loud and clear.

But, the tumult over "educating for a life" and "training for a job" persists; in the case of journalism it will be heightened as long as huge national corporations, driven by their bottom-line mentalities, continue to dominate truth-seeking and truth-telling in communities from Kentucky to New York and California, especially in newsrooms where "freedom of the press" is widely understood as "freedom of the press to do anything it wishes without accountability." One of the major problems confronting journalism today is its simplistic, built-in arrogance, its self-righteous beliefs reinforced behind its own closed doors.

There is an answer.

Individuals should return to individualism based upon morality. If journalists have a mandate from the First Amendment, so private scribes of every kind have an equal right. The trouble in the last years of this troubled 20th century is that too many individuals have forfeited their birthrights and have allowed themselves to be too narrowly trained for "jobs" (including journalism). A nation and a world of individuals should find a common ground, the most fertile of meeting places, in the enrichment of liberal arts education, which should begin in the home where responsibilities lie in the hands of parents.

The Smile

"The smiles that win, the tints that glow
but tell of days in goodness spent,
a mind at peace with all below."

– Lord Byron –

*T*he student sat across the desk from me, his advisor at the
university.

"I'm thinking of leaving computer science."

"To do what?"

"To become a disc jockey, maybe."

I rested the back of my head in my folded hands, remembering
how long ago I'd said the same thing about leaving cryptography in
the U.S. Navy to become a world-class deejay flying high in
Southern California. For me, neither extreme had been a very good
idea.

"Why leave computer science? Are you burned out?"

The student smiled as if to say it was a possibility. The student had
a kind smile. It was a gentleness so often missing in the rush to
advise and be advised. "I should like for you to consider the
possibility of *not* studying journalism," I carefully asserted.

"What do you recommend?"

"Oh, I don't know. What about music?"

The student smiled again. There was something about the smile
that was compelling. It was genuine as well as gentle.

"What brings you to journalism, anyway?" I asked.

"I could read the news. I would like to read the news."

"They do that in a few places, read the news on radio—England,
for example—but generally speaking, in this country there are few
news readers." (I remembered the late Douglas Edwards, the pre-

eminent news reader for CBS News Radio and Television.)

The student expressed interest and listened very carefully. Listening was something this student demonstrated remarkably well. After all, listening—real, honest-to-goodness listening—seems headed for the endangered species list. Here was a student who smiled beautifully and listened carefully. I explained the importance of aggressive, yet sensitive on-the-spot reporting as well as the need for clear writing to satisfy the diverse needs of a mass audience.

"I don't see you doing that kind of reporting. I mean, I think you would have a very hard time doing it, competitively."

The student nodded agreement, but the smile did not vanish. The desire to listen did not seem to diminish. The student leaned forward in his chair, eager for good advice. I hoped I was providing it.

"I should think the College of Fine Arts might have what you need—music, in particular. By the way, what kind of music do you like?"

"All kinds. But, popular music, mostly—top forty."

"Well, then, what I suggest you do is stay in computer science while looking for that job in radio. Or, you might move over to Fine Arts and study music while looking for that disc jockey job. I'll be happy to make a phone call for you."

The phone call was made. The contact suggested that the student call the following day for a name and number in Louisville. The advisor wrote the information on a piece of paper and handed it to the student. The student smiled and rose to go. He said he would make the call.

Usually, the advisor does not rise to see students to the door. Hardly ever does he walk all the way to the front door. Almost never does he walk outside with the students to be sure they are safely on their way.

This student did not need help. He walked confidently down the winding stairs of the journalism building. When he reached the bottom step, he turned right and *ran* joyously down the well-worn concrete path taken by hundreds of thousands of other students over the years.

This student was almost unique. He had never stopped smiling. He had never stopped listening.

And now, as he ran, the student's Seeing Eye dog ran behind him, as if knowing it was good for the youth to cut loose and let his joy show for all the world to see.

Needles and Threads

"And gladly wolde he lerne, and gladly teche."
— Geoffrey Chaucer —

*T*he needle's eye...was the school teacher. And the thread that ran
so true could only be play*." Jesse wrote that 45 years ago. A
pilgrimage to his beloved W-Hollow was long overdue, so I *played*
and headed east on Interstate 64. It was almost instant relief to turn
north on KY 1 at Grayson to follow the Little Sandy River through
Pactolas, seven miles to Oldtown and eight more miles to Argillite
near the meeting of the Little Sandy and its East Fork. The twisting
two-lane road was bowered with many of Jesse's favorite trees: Gum
and Oak, with Pines pointing toward the sky. There was coolness
beneath the greenery—Greenup County was rightly named.

W-Hollow was named for good reason too. KY 2433 winds
between KY 1 and KY 2 like Ws end on end. The split rail fence at
Jesse's place has mellowed, but it holds on as if it were put there to
stay. I looked at the house and wondered about the joys of living
Jesse and Naomi had shared. A young man directed me to their final
resting place. I wanted to go there and stand at the edge of that spot
for a while as the day sank beneath the hills; I wanted to stand on the
rim of peace at the center and catch a glimpse inside if that were
possible.

Plum Grove Cemetery is just across the road from the New Life
Baptist Church. I had to ask several times before I found it. By now,
Jesse had to be smiling.

"You go up that hill and down that hill and up another hill and
down that one to where those two house trailers are and you turn
left," said a man seated outside his father's house, the father nodding

that it was so.

"Plum Grove? It's right up that holler there," pointed a lady relaxing in a front porch swing.

"Yes, it's on up there at the top of the hill," said a young girl who had run out into her yard to gather up a puppy.

Plum Grove Cemetery was a high clearing surrounded by wooded hills, and the monument for a teacher who became a poet and novelist stood near the center:

Jesse Hilton Stuart
August 8, 1906
February 17, 1984
Naomi Deane Norris Stuart

Naomi's grave hadn't grassed over, because she was buried beside Jesse in the summer of '93. I'd wanted to go to her funeral, but maybe she and Jesse understood I was committed to teaching at a writer's workshop at the University of Kentucky. Jesse's monument is filled with words from his writings, and I was made to feel humble as I read:

> *No one can ever tell me that education, rightly directed*
> *without propaganda, cannot change the individual,*
> *community, county, state, and the world for the better. It can...*
> *and I am firm in my belief that a teacher lives on and on*
> *through his sudents... Good teaching is Forever and the*
> *teacher is immortal.*

I went to the other side:

> *Now look, my friends—look to the east and west... This land*
> *is mine. I sing it to you ... This land is mine, for I am part of*
> *it. I am the land, for it is part of me—we are akin and thus*
> *our kinship be! It would make me a brother to the tree! And*
> *far as eyes can see this land is mine. Not for one foot of it I*

have a deed—to own this land I do not need a deed—they all belong to me—gum, oak and pine.

An Oak planted a decade ago grows strong and well at Jesse's feet:

What is life worth when he take and don't give? And when the best in us will not awaken?... Should not man look to morning for his light before the body fails, his life is wasted?

I turned and watched the light of day declining to the west. I looked a last time at the hallowed place and said, "Thank you, Jesse ... And thank you, Naomi."

Back on KY 1, I stopped again at Earl's house, he who had nodded agreement with his son's directions to Plum Grove Cemetery. I sat beside 72-year-old Earl and asked him what he thought of Jesse.

"Knew him all my life. He bought two mules, Erf and Jad, from my daddy and my granddaddy. He mentioned them in *Man With a Bull-Tongued Plow*. He changed Erf's name to Hearsh."

"Did Jesse laugh a lot?"

"He laughed and smiled. He was honest and worked hard. He walked many miles to school. Everybody looked up to him. He was a mighty fine man."

If I were not the eye of the needle this day, if I were not the center through which peace had passed, I was very close. And the thread running so true through me was the *play* I had felt in coming to know Jesse and Naomi and the role of the educator and the educated better than I ever had before.

The Teacher

"Let's teach ourselves."

— William Shakespeare –

*T*en years of teaching at the college level will be enough to last me for the rest of my life. The student evaluations of my teaching have been a mixture of positive enthusiasm and unabashed anger. There was one semester when I thought I'd done my best, my very best: I'd prepared for each class, carefully constructed the lectures, returned written assignments in a timely manner, and had maintained an open-door policy and had given everybody who walked through, the most honest and sympathetic mentoring of which I was capable.. One student wrote: "This man should never teach again as long as he lives."

In time I concluded that if only 80% of my students approved of my courses and the way I taught them, I should not be dismayed. Yes, it hurt to realize that simple arithmatic showed 20% disliked me and my methods, but I quickly learned and had come to accept the reality that if teaching is anything at all, it is a humbling experience.

Early one morning in my office at the University of Kentucky, when I was grading papers for a class of more than 100 students, I said to myself, "Do you realize that if you are *really* good at this, the administration would pay you to do it until you drop in your tracks? Do you realize that if you are *really* good at this, you could be using the time to grade *yourself*? Instead of correcting the papers of others, you could be correcting your own; instead of critiquing others' writing, you could be spending the best years of your life fully engaged in your own creativity. Your writing might be good, it might be bad, it might fall somewhere in the middle — but it would be your *OWN*!

It was this kind of soul-searching that led to my decision to attempt to leave teaching and to begin to think and write as if my life depended on it. I would become the student, the learner, the experimenter and all I would ever expect of myself would be to do the best I could at any moment of the day.

PART FIVE

Liberty

Wake-up Call

"We classify disease as error, which nothing but
Truth or Mind can heal."

– Mary Baker Eddy –

*T*he ride on the gurney through the passageways of the University of Kentucky Medical Center to the operating room seemed faster than necessary, but by then there were enough sedatives and pain killers juicing in my body that it was rather fun seeing staff members ducking out of the way, disappearing through doors as if to escape a runaway streetcar.

My wave goodbye to Lalie standing on the edge of the pre-op area had been nothing much more than a weak flutter of my left arm. She probably had blown me a kiss, but I can't remember whether I'd had the energy to blow one back to her as we'd done so many times during the past 20 years of sharing innermost secrets, feelings, or apprehensions about all the unknowns lurking around the darkest corners of our lives.

Reverend Cliff Pike had held my hand and prayed for me. It was a simple prayer and it felt good to hear it.

On a recent day I had said aloud to myself:

"You either believe in the Lord or you don't—which is it?"

Without hesitation, I had replied to myself:

"I believe in the Lord."

"Well then, if you believe in the Lord, and he wants you to come Home today, how could you say, 'No'?"

"If He wants me to come Home today, I'm ready," I answered calmly.

And later, I'd be reminded by Howell Raines, the Alabama-born journalist, in his fine book on fly-fishing, the battle cry of the Cheyenne Indians: "It's a good day to die!"

My arrival in the operating room was unheralded, not exactly Local Boy Makes Good, Returns Home For Joyous Celebration—the nurses and other attendants were probably thinking, if not sighing, well, here he is. He waited until the last possible second, never taking seriously all that's been said over and over again about "early detection," so it's time to go to work to try to save one more who should have known better.

"Mr. Dick, we want you just to scoot off of this bed onto this table," said the voice belonging to the conductor of the runaway streetcar.

I maneuvered my knees, my rear end, and the heels of my feet, and the next to last thing I remember was lowering down on the spot where they wanted me to be.

"Just one more little scoot...that's fine...you're just right," said the voice a final time.

It must've been then that the lights went out in Georgia. My old friend Janet White, the anesthesiologist who wore her beeper pager at the Communion rail, must've dropped a couple of cannonballs into the I.V., because from then until the surgeon had cut me open, removed the lymph nodes and sent them for biopsy, made the determination that the cancer was most probably confined to the prostate, stitched me back up again, and returned me to the recovery room, I knew absolutely nothing, felt absolutely nothing, might as well've been wearing wings and flying outside the pearly gates.

"Merry Christmas—the lymph nodes were negative," said the voice of the head surgeon, Dr. William McRoberts, considered one of the finest urologists in the nation, his face carrying a broad, encouraging smile. The attending physician, Dr. Steven Jensen, was smiling his youthful smile without reservation.

"Thank you," I'd like to believe I mumbled.

From the Tuesday of the operation to the following Saturday when I was dismissed from the Lucille Parker Markey Cancer Center, I gave thanks, thanks that I'd been so fortunate as to have gone in for such a simple blood test as the PSA—possibly the best indicator we presently have of whether there's a malignancy in the prostate. I'd been told, if I'd not gone in when I did I probably would have been dead in about a year and a half.

Talk about wake-up calls!

As I write in May, following my 64th birthday in February, I've finished the maximum 39 radiation treatments, each including 15 seconds of calibrated radiation beams through my left side, 15 seconds through my front side, 15 seconds through my right side, and 15 seconds through my backside. Two months after the last radiation therapy, my PSA level had dropped from the 60s to the 20s, and when Dr. McRoberts examined me he said my prostate felt "lovely." I asked him if it were O.K. for my mind to be telling me that I feel so good. He said there is statistical evidence that the mind plays a positive part in the curing of disease.

The death in May of Jackie Kennedy Onassis shook me terribly. The reliving of Camelot and what seemed to be the dying of it, again, threw me into a tailspin of remorse. One night, I had a nightmare and in it, Dr. McRoberts was telling me that it was all over for me, that I'd have to return for surgery and that nothing looked good. That same night, I dreamed I was a reporter for CBS News in France, and everybody knew there was going to be a gigantic train wreck. The news media went out to cover it. I saw the train coming in the distance. It was traveling at a high rate of speed. In the middle of the small town where we were gathered, directly in front of me, the track buckled, the train heaved and people began spilling out. Suddenly, firing squads were shooting survivors. I began running. I ran as hard and as fast as my legs would carry me. When I woke up, I was headed back to the bathroom.

I scheduled another, earlier appointment with Dr. McRoberts. I told him of all my fears. He listened, and I could feel the compassion showing on his face. He examined me and said, "Perfectly benign!"

I asked him if I now could tell my friends, "I'm in remission!"

"We'll wait and see the results of the PSA on Friday."

On the last day of May, I was told that the blood test reading had dropped another six points. The fat person had not yet sung.

I know there are no guarantees, and I know that my body, just as the body of Mary Baker Eddy, will die one day. It could be today, it could be tomorrow. But, one day it will happen. And it will be at that moment when my soul will be set free to soar with the ages. Even though the doctors say they believe they can cure me of this silent, killer disease that appeared out of nowhere (with the only symptoms being getting up to go to the bathroom several times during the night), will I be inspired to pray for the health of my *soul*? That is the better question.

Everything else about me—heart, liver, gall bladder, lungs, and nervous system—is just fine. I'm overweight, no doubt about that, stubborn as a mule, no question there either, and obviously not half as smart as I imagine I am. I didn't even know the difference between the colon and the prostate! And I'd not heard of the PSA test (the only way I can remember it now is as short for "Public Service Announcement").

Maybe that's what this is, a public service announcement. If you're a male and over forty, if you love your family and figure they need you around during the most productive years of your life, if you care about yourself even a little bit, go have a specialist, a urologist, perform the simplest of examinations. If you're lucky it'll cost relatively little. If you need treatment, it'll still be less expensive than the loss to yourself and your family.

Cancer of the prostate is a genuine puzzler. They're still looking for the cause. Dr. Jensen took a sample of my bone marrow to contribute to the ongoing research at the Kentucky Clinic and the Albert Benjamin Chandler Medical Center. One day, they're going to find the cause for this and many other diseases. In the meantime, I hope to be around, cheering you on, building up your confidence, holding your hand as my wife and family and friends held mine and tell you as they kept telling me, "It's going to be all right!"

Mailcall

"The strength of criticism lies in the weakness
of the thing criticized."

– Henry Wadsworth Longfellow –

A much appreciated letter arrived the other day. Since it was signed, "Respectfully," I'd like to answer it in the same spirit. The letter had begun: "Regarding 'The View from Plum Lick,' (my monthly column In *Kentucky Living* magazine) you don't always follow the plumb line but show each month a definite leftist liberal tilt."

Putting a label on me at this time in my life just doesn't wear well. But, to tell the truth, it's pretty much a toss-up as to whether I'm "conservative" or "liberal." I'm conservative on pornography. I intend to protect my seven-year-old child from it as long as I'm able. (This promptly fetched a letter from a "liberal" accusing me of associating liberalism with pornography, which of course was never intended, but some folks wear their liberal hearts pretty much out on their sleeves, and I can't worry about something I'm powerless to control.)

On the matter of helping thousands of Kurds dying of starvation in the mountains along the border between Iraq and Turkey, I was liberal. On the question of whether to force Saddam Hussein to remove himself and his forces from Kuwait, I was entirely in favor of it. Whether that gives me a liberal tilt or a conservative tilt, I'm not sure, since most people in the United States supported the Gulf War, and we didn't fuss at each other about what we ought to call ourselves.

On the issue of the Civil War in our own country, I put more stock in Abraham Lincoln than I do Jefferson Davis, both of them Kentuckians born and bred. This will come as no surprise to my mother-in-law as well as my child's godfather in Mississippi, who, with a lot of other good folks down there, see it the other way around. If it hadn't been for Jefferson Davis, I wouldn't have met my southern belle wife, who as it turns out is conservative on pornography and liberal on Kurds, too. The letter criticizing me pointed out: "David Dick talks about Security and Freedom and yet...he delights in savaging George Wallace, who was hardly allowed first amendment freedom of speech on some of our campuses."

The last part of that was correct. I was with George Wallace when bricks as well as rotten eggs were thrown at him. I didn't like it any more than he did. I was with him in the shopping center in Laurel, Maryland, and I was very lucky that I was not hit by the bullets that brought the Governor down.

It should come as no surprise that George Wallace was both conservative and liberal, and he didn't like political labels any more than I do. He was a conservative when he stood in the schoolhouse door; he was a liberal when years later after his stand he crowned the Black homecoming queen at the same University of Alabama. Have I "savaged" Governor Wallace? Anyone has a first amendment right to say I have (that's an idea based on liberal interpretation of a Bill of Rights born of libertarianism). I hope I haven't "savaged" anybody, including Governor Wallace. I hope all I've done is to report as much as possible and as fairly and as accurately as possible about any public figure I've ever covered.

I knew Governor Wallace didn't think I was out to savage him when one day in southern Alabama he invited me to join him in the back room of a country store to eat sardines on crackers. One of my private, treasured photographs shows us two good old boys enjoying ourselves, while being liberal with the hot sauce and conservative with the crackers.

As for all the truth being important, Governor Wallace used to say out on the campaign trail: "If anybody ever tells you they've got the whole truth and nothing but the truth, so help them God, you better watch 'em cause they're about to do something to you."

Freedom

"I know but one freedom and that is
the freedom of the mind."

— Antoine de Saint-Exupére –

*F*reedom: one of those words that means pretty much what the writer or the speaker or the rascal believes or says it means, which is what causes most of the problem. I've just about decided that there's little if any freedom anywhere on the face of this earth, and as far as that goes, I tend to believe that freedom in Heaven or Hell will be well managed by both the good and the bad forces if you want to know the unvarnished truth about it.

I read in the *New York Times* a few years back that the forces who staged a coup in the Philippines did so because the general who led it said what they wanted was "real" freedom, suggesting of course that there is such a thing as unreal freedom, which to me sounds a great deal like what I'm talking about. It appears to me that "real freedom" is just about as unreal as plain old "freedom," and to add another word to it is a waste of time.

The sad and tragic fact is that people (especially young people at the direction of older people) are regularly asked to lay down their lives for the cause of freedom. It's amazing how relatively easy it is to enlist so many people, train them, and send them out as "freedom fighters." In Nicaragua, the Contras have been the freedom fighters, while in Managua, the Sandinistas who started out as freedom fighters against General Somoza are still jealously guarding "freedom" throughout the freedom-ravaged nation, and Somoza went to his grave believing that all the time he was the freedom father figure.

Then there have been the freedom fighters in Afghanistan. Naturally, they're engaged in mortal combat because they believe the Russians don't know the first thing about freedom, the same Russians who overthrew the czars because they didn't know diddly about freedom, and if the czars couldn't comprehend it, how in the name of peace could an illiterate peasant in Afghanistan be expected to figure it out?

Which brings me to the Alamo.

I never go to San Antonio that I don't look at the Alamo or visit it if there's time, because I've never grown tired of walking where Davy Crockett, William Travis, Jim Bowie, and James Bonham lived the final moments of their courageous, freedom-loving lives. I've never taken kindly to any theories that what they really were was a bunch of raging, certified crazies. They had plenty of chances to get out of that hell hole. As James Michener has described it in *Texas,* Bonham in particular seemed almost to be making a game out of seeing how many times he could break through enemy lines to go looking for help. The 182 Texas freedom fighters had held out for days against as awesome a set of bad odds as one would ever dread. Yet, the martyrs had all apparently been convinced that they would rather die than surrender to General Santa Anna's idea concerning freedom.

Say what you will about Antonio Lopez de Santa Anna (and there is certainly a great deal to be lamented about his reputation for killing, burning, and pillaging), he was after all trying to hold on to

his own nation. He didn't think Crockett, Travis, Bowie, Bonham or any number of "freedom fighters" from Kentucky or Tennessee or anyplace else in the freedom-loving gringo world deserved to be treated with an ounce of southern hospitality so long as what they really wanted to do was to take his land away from him and the government he represented. Santa Anna hated these "invaders" with a vengeance as savage as any ever recorded in the long history of people engaged in another give-me-freedom-or-give-me-death struggle.

William Barret Travis' final dispatch to the world (included in Michener's *Texas*) is as poignant and tragic and courageous and important as any I've ever had the privilege to read on a hot, quiet Sunday afternoon in the shadows of the immortalized Alamo.

> *To the People of Texas and All Americans in the world.*
> *Fellow Citizens and Compatriots. I am besieged by a*
> *thousand or more of the Mexicans under Santa Anna...The*
> *enemy has demanded a surrender at discretion, otherwise, the*
> *garrison are to be put to the sword, if the fort is taken, I have*
> *answered the demand with a cannon shot, and our flag still*
> *waves proudly from the walls. I shall never surrender or*
> *retreat...I call on you in the name of Liberty, or patriotism*
> *and everything dear to the American character, to come to*
> *our aid, with all dispatch ... If this call is neglected I am*
> *determined to sustain myself as long as possible and die like*
> *a soldier who never forgets what is due his honor and that of*
> *his country.*
> *Victory or Death.*

On the early morning of March 6, 1836, it was death for the defenders of the Alamo. Soon after, it would be defeat for General Santa Anna at the Battle of San Jacinto, where General Sam Houston had his revenge, again in the name of "freedom." Santa Anna, who had scaled the heights of fastidiousness by carrying a silver chamber pot wherever he fought his battles, had finally been out-foxed, out-maneuvered, and out-freedomed by a motley bunch of Kentuckians, Tennesseans, and others, hardly any of whom had a pot to freedom in.

That's the way it is whenever the magic word freedom is invoked. It depends on whose freedom one is talking about (or trying to steal). It's a little like saying, just a spoonful of freedom makes the medicine go down. It might do wonders for credibility if we weren't quite so pious about our own freedom declarations. "Western Expansion" and "Manifest Destiny" are rather poor substitutes for "Imperialism" and "Death to the Savages."

Freedom is a beautiful and complex idea that should not be cheapened or bastardized or confused with real world intentions.

On the Road with Charles Kuralt

"On the back roads of America,
I felt at home at last."

– Charles Kuralt –

*C*harles Kuralt and a former colleague were "on the road" from the Singletary Center for the Arts at the University of Kentucky to the Alumni House across the street. It was a short stroll, yet time enough to ponder the events of the Spring of '89—the dedication of the First Amendment Center in the Journalism Building, and Charles' exquisite delivery of the annual Joe Creason Lecture. It had been a splendid defense of the First Amendment.

"But you know, Charles, I think the First Amendment probably wouldn't receive enough votes to pass today."

"I think you're right," sighed the troubled Kuralt, who had caused to be remembered on this day the many journalists killed in Argentina because they had dared to tell the truth.

"Sometimes, the First Amendment drives me crazy," Charles had said during the lecture, but then had added, "What is worse is silence."

"There aren't many things for which I'd be willing to die, but the First Amendment is one of them," the former colleague had said earlier in the day. The wiser journalist, who had flown in from North Carolina, had smiled acknowledgement, but had declined to engage in bravado. It wasn't necessary. Kuralt's instinctive understanding of the most fundamental of democratic concepts was unmistakable. He knew well the words; *"Congress shall make no law ... abridging the freedom of speech, or of the press...."*

Charles Kuralt, the "On the Road" journalist who would retire from CBS in 1994, whose range of subject matter had stretched from "swimming pigs" in Texas to an interview with the Pope in the Vatican, recalled the inauguration of the first President of the United States, the revolutionary who could have been King but chose to be President. There was a nation, but as yet there was no Bill of Rights, and it would be Thomas Jefferson who would catch a new breath of freedom in France. He wrote in 1787:

> *The people are the only censors of their governors... The way to prevent these irregular interpositions of the people, is to give them full information of their affairs through the channel of the public papers, and to contrive that those papers should penetrate the whole mass of the people. The basis of our government being the opinion of the people, the very first object should be to keep that right; and were it left to me to decide whether we should have a government without newspapers, or newspapers without a government, I should not hesitate a moment to prefer the latter.*

Whether it be left to us to decide whether we should have a government without a Charles Kuralt, or a Charles Kuralt without a government is equally an oversimplification, yet one not without merit or appeal. Although this remains a nation of laws, not men, any nation of laws without a Charles Kuralt is not only the poorer, but one with a certain tendency toward authoritarianism, and at the same time, it leaves a network the poorer with a certain tendency toward glitz. (It also makes it vulnerable to a Rupert Murdock and his Fox Network.)

On Easter Sunday 1994, Charles Kuralt appeared for the last time on CBS's "Sunday Morning." I wrote the following words about his retirement, which appeared on the op-ed page of the *Lexington Herald-Leader*.

"Charles Kuralt once said, 'Don't tell them, but I'd pay them to let me work here.' The irony is that Charles would probably *have* to pay them if he were to show up for a job today. Even then it's doubtful he would be hired—he's too overweight, too bald, and too slow, although he's certainly in good company in the maturing process.

"Eric Sevareid was eventually removed from the CBS Evening News because his commentaries were too long—two to three minutes of rare wisdom—an eternity and an anomoly on a network news broadcast. Walter Cronkite was wise in stepping aside when he did, for he was becoming an increasingly fusty father figure. Bill Moyers' brilliant documentaries became ill-suited for the four-second sound bite fragmentations that came to pass for broadcast 'journalism,' and he had the good sense to return to PBS.

"The retirement of Charles Kuralt becomes one of the last, lost chunks of quality at CBS News, the Tiffany Network that in the minds of many has increasingly become the Diffident Network. The sensitivity and humanity of Charles Kuralt, whose college education was in American Studies, have made him a national treasure, but the sad reality is that he is no longer a role model for young broadcast journalists who identify more naturally with the quick-and-dirty, junkyard dog mentality and manners that have come to exemplify the broadcast 'journalist' of the 1990s.

"A recent *TV Guide* cover displays Diane Sawyer (Charles Kuralt's one-time co-anchor on the CBS Morning News) looking more like a fashion model than a journalist. The story was about her new $7-million contract. In the same issue, *TV Guide's* 'Jeers' included a reference to Sawyer's interview with Charles Manson and a woman who described what it was like stabbing to death the pregnant Sharon Tate. (Diane Sawyer is a splendidly unique journalist and posing in fancy clothes never seemed necessary for her.)

"Years ago, a CBS producer admonished a young reporter who objected to the use of irrelevant, bizarre pictures in a story:

'The trouble with you is you need to get some tabloid in your blood.' With the passing of time has come the greatest arterial rupture of tabloid 'news' since the days of William Randolph Hearst and Joseph Pulitzer at the peak of the yellow journalism days of the late 19th century.

"Kuralt's 'On the Road' magic suffered by contrast with such punched-up hard news segments as Dan Rather's '48 Hours,' Connie Chung's 'Eye to Eye,' and the designated hitter's 'Reality Check.' It appears to one CBS retiree that CBS News could use an occasional 'Reality Check' of its own. Wouldn't that be fun? But would the skin of the cast of characters be thick enough to stand it? Doubtful.

"'Sunday Morning' with Charles Kuralt standing there in his loosely fitting suit, or sitting there talking really intelligently with a correspondent in the field, or not being there at all while the natural sounds of birds or running streams filled the audio track and pulled the viewer into a unique relationship with nature—that was the stuff of which Peabody Awards were earned.

"Charles Kuralt was in Lexington, Kentucky, twice in recent years. He met with college students and faculty, and what you saw was what you got—a gentle, quiet man of compassion, intellect and the joy of not taking one's self as seriously as most of the present generation of 'anchor' people.

"During one of his visits, Kuralt spoke with me about the likelihood of his retirement from CBS News. He indicated it was soon forthcoming, and he said he wanted to spend more time writing. Could as much be imagined of the high profile news personalities who measure their annual income in the multi-millions of dollars? Doubtful.

"We're going to miss Charles on 'Sunday Morning' (whose own future now becomes uncertain at best), just as we've missed him 'On the Road'." But then, perhaps there'll be many new chapters of writings by Charles Kuralt, and for that his fans will be forever in his debt.

Reflections on Milton's Areopagitica and the First Amendment

"A good idea would be for every family to get the Constitution
and read the first 10 amendments out loud."

– Ralph McGill –

We the people of the United States, in Order to form a more perfect Union, establish justice, insure domestic Tranquility, provide for the common defence, promote the general Welfare, and secure the blessings of Liberty to ourselves and our Posterity, do ordain and establish this Constitution for the United States of America.

This great preamble resounds throughout the land, across the generations of 200 years. It has become so much a part of us, the terrible temptation is to take it for granted—or ignore it altogether. We do so at our greatest peril, for on that day, September 17, 1787, when all 12 state delegations approved the Constitution of the United States, there was set in motion a plan, an outline for national life. It would become more than a prescription for survival. It was a logical, compassionate, innovative design for dignity and democracy.

The idea of separated powers providing checks and balances was to become our inheritance. Without that philosophy we would have been no better off than any other fiefdom, any other colony, any other dependance. If the Constitution were to be the blueprint for our governance—giving structure to the inspiration of the Declaration of Independence of 1776—it would be the Bill of Rights in 1791 that would raise the Constitution to true and lasting greatness. One need not be a journalist to appreciate the First Amendment to the Constitution of the United States of America.

Each time we pray, or choose not to pray, or choose not to believe in praying, we owe thanks to the First Amendment.

Each time we make an utterance, no matter how disagreeable to the powers that be, we should know it is the First Amendment that makes it possible.

Each time we gather in a room or on a street corner or on a creek bank with peaceful intent, it is the First Amendment that guarantees the right to do so.

Each time we petition the government because we believe ourselves to be wronged, it is the First Amendment that allows us to step forward and plead our case.

Each time we roll the presses or transmit through the medium of broadcasting, it is the First Amendment, that frees us from mad or even benign interference.

It serves no real purpose to argue about the relative order of the guarantees of the First Amendment. They are all there, and each has its unique considerations and consequences. Let others debate the importance of there being no law respecting an establishment of religion, or prohibiting the free exercise thereof; let others weigh the significance of all else in the First Amendment; it is the certain duty of journalists to guard and attempt to explain the value of freedom of the press. In fact, it should be everyone's work, but if it not be the special responsibility of journalists, then freedom as we know it is left hanging over cliffs of no return.

Freedom of the press makes it legitimate for us to be about our country's business. Our commission is to seek the truth and to tell the truth. Too many of the press's critics decry the fact that it is impossible, certainly unrealistic to expect anybody, journalists included, to hang out the whole truth to dry on the clotheslines of our newspapers, magazines, and broadcast facilities. The detractors know better, or should if they don't, but that doesn't prevent them from going after this main artery of the First Amendment as best it seems to serve their selfish purposes.

All any journalist or teacher or preacher can do, or ought to be expected to do, is to present as accurately as possible as much of the truth as is presently available. Bits and pieces of the truth are far better than anything masquerading as a grand and totally flawless "truth." Yet it's probably long overdue that journalists have something to say that quietens rather than quickens. Too much is made of competition and vanity, as if we didn't have enough of both already.

No student has yet to take me up on my standing invitation to come down to the farm here on Plum Lick, to walk alone to the top of the hill, there to read Milton's *Areopagitica*, his magnificent tributes to truth. Nonetheless, if I do no more than encourage all youth to take this priceless book down from the shelf and read some small portion of it, I will consider my task as an educator sufficiently undertaken. The *Areopagitica* was a part of that warm and loamy 17th century soil where the roots of the First Amendment in the Bill of Rights to the Constitution of the United States of America reach down deeply for sustenance.

> *...when complaints are freely heard, deeply considered, and speedily reformed, then is the utmost bound of civil liberty attained that wise men look for.*

> *As good almost kill a man as kill a good book: who kills a man kills a reasonable creature, God's image; but he who destroys a good book, kills reason itself, kills the image of God, as it were in the eye.*

> *...I cannot praise a fugitive and cloistered virtue, unexercised and unbreathed, that never sallies out and sees her adversary, but slinks out of the race, where that immortal garland is to be run for, not without dust and heat. Assuredly we bring not innocence into the world, we bring impurity much rather: that which purifies us is trial, and trial is by what is contrary.*

Where there is much desire to learn, there of necessity will be much arguing, much writing, many opinions; for opinion in good men is but knowledge in the making.

Give me the liberty to know, to utter, and to argue freely according to conscience, above all liberties.

Though all the winds of doctrine were let loose to play upon the earth, so Truth be in the field, we do injuriously by licensing and prohibiting to misdoubt her strength. Let her and Falsehood grapple; who ever knew Truth put to the worse, in a free and open encounter.

Happy Birthday!

I was born on July 4, 1776, and the Declaration
of Independence is my birth certificate....
I am the nation. I am 213 million living souls—
and the ghost of millions who have lived and died for me."

— Otto Whittaker —

A member of the Plum Lick family is celebrating a birthday in July. Because we take all our birthdays right seriously here in the valley where the normally tiny Plum Lick Creek runs through, it seems only proper to remember this person with special gratitude for all the good things we've received as a result of this individual's "being there" when needed. For instance, when we woke up to the early, refreshing coolness of morning in the summer of 1994, we didn't have to worry about enemy armies coming across the lovely western hills, whose contoured shapes are like a beautiful woman sleeping. When we turn on the radio and listen to the reports coming from National Public Radio, we have no reason to doubt the independence of the messages. Of course, the NPR "complaint line" is sprinkled with criticisms but they are examples of Milton's *"...liberty to know, to utter, and to argue freely according to conscience."*

We're confident that there has been no censorship by the federal government or any TPITDTU (The Public Is Too Dumb To Understand) Office, or a STSDLDFT (Since They're So Dumb Let's Decide For Them) agency.

The First Amendment to the Constitution is as alive and well in July as it was in June, as it will be in August, as it was last year, as it most likely will be next year:

Congress shall make no law respecting an establishment of

religion, or prohibiting the free exercise thereof; or abridging the freedom of speech, or of the press; or the right of the people peaceably to assemble, and to petition the government for a redress of grievances.

Those 45 words are the stuff of which truly great birthday cakes are baked. It includes the cake, the filling, and the frosting on top; and most cooking experts would be hard-pressed to come up with a better recipe for freedom. When the Constitution of the United States of America was ratified in 1788, it was believed to need basic guarantees for individual liberty, and they were added. The First Amendment addressed freedom of expression; the Second and Third Amendments provided protections in relation to arms and troops; the Fourth through the Eighth Amendments granted rights to accused persons; and the Ninth and Tenth Amendments dealt with the rights of people and states. Taken as a body, these ten amendments have constituted the American Bill of Rights, and without it we would be both impoverished and threatened as we live out our lives along the creek leading to the sea.

Our birthday child is adding one more important candle in a year that has witnessed more chaos and atrocities in what used to be Yugoslavia, where a brutal civil war has been a mammoth rape of body, mind, and spirit—a new term, "ethnic cleansing," has entered the languages of the world, and it is an insult to all mankind. The situation is even more horrifying in Rwanda in central Africa. Although there can be no offsetting, no balancing out of these cataclysms, there is a promise of multi-racial democracy in South Africa with the election of the formerly imprisoned Nelson Mandela.

It has also been the year of the trial of the survivors of the Branch Davidian catastrophe, made all the more difficult to condemn because its roots go back to the same *"Congress shall make no law respecting an establishment of religion, or prohibiting the free exercise thereof..."*

The individual whose birthday we celebrate is best known for precisely that characteristic—*individualism*—which sets us apart from most other nations in the world. It may not be an overstatement to say a community is no stronger than its weakest individual. As we light the candles for our birthday guest, it would be in our collective community's best interest to rededicate ourselves to more committed individualism in all matters of body and soul. It is important to know ourselves in order that we might know better our neighbors. The knowing should come of honest considerations, and "face saving" should be among the least of our concerns. It seems to make a great deal of sense to identify our strengths and use them for ourselves and the free community in which we live.

The cake is baked. The wind beneath the Maple trees is right for lighting the candles. The individual whose day we celebrate is present and ready to be honored. The 218 candles are lit and burning brightly. It is time to make a national wish—perhaps, it is an expression of hope for peace, prosperity, a more perfect union, the continuance of justice and domestic tranquility. Most of us understand that most worthwhile things don't "just happen." All good outcomes require dedicated, inspired, persistent effort. Praying can't hurt; in fact, without it there's a hollow ring to the best of celebrations.

"Happy Birthday, Uncle Sam!"

PART SIX

High Tide

Final Arrangements

"Man with the burning soul
Has but an hour of breath
To build a ship of truth
On which his soul may sail—"

– John Masefield –

*W*ell, we had put it off as long as possible, until we figured there was no rhyme nor reason to delay any longer. Feeling older, true, yet optimistic about the future, we sat down with our funeral director to make our final arrangements. We had dreaded it as much as most folks doubtless do, but we kept coming back to the idea that dying and what to do about mortal remains are the responsibility of the person who is the main participant. Leaving the grim business to loved ones or total strangers had always seemed to us to be considerably irresponsible. Loved ones will be spared much unnecessary agony, and total strangers won't give a whoop one way or the other.

As for myself, I'd given some thought to cremation, but I finally ruled it out after considering certain aspects of it. When I was a child I had memorized the "Cremation of Sam McGee" and it stuck in my brain along with my social security number.

The words had made a lasting and mostly negative impression on me. Oh, it was pretty funny until I became much older. Even the last lines of Robert Service's poem—*"And there sat Sam, looking cool and calm in the heat of the furnace roar"*—not even those words did I find comforting when applied to myself at final arrangements time. So, I opted for mold'ring in the grave.

Besides, if I were cremated it would seem only right to have something to say in advance about the disposition of the ashes. Being on somebody's mantlepiece or in somebody's safe deposit box or even in the ground held neither special nor cooling appeal for me. There was a moment when I thought it would be rather nice to be scattered over the farm from a plane. Fine, but at what time of day? If it were sunrise then my loved one would probably spend a restless night on the eve of the event. If it were sunset, then she would have all day to fret about it. If it were high noon, I'd probably be remembered for showboating to the end.

Who could fault mold'ring?

It was time to talk about the whole thing with the undertaker. Actually, they don't seem to like that term as much as they used to. "Funeral Arranger" or "Funeral Director" is preferred for the same reason that "cemetery" replaced "graveyard" and "memorial garden" has taken its place in the patois of the funeral parlor, the usual somber business of burying folks. In any event, instead of going to the funeral "home," we invited him and his wife to our place. Sitting at the head of one's own table affords one a much more commanding position and at least there one feels more comfortable and confident about directing the conversation, if not the afterlife.

We proceeded through the before-dinner drinks, the white wine with the seafood salad, the main course gumbo, the pecan pie à la mode, and the brandy in the coffee, without once mentioning the hereafter. Symbolically, it might have been considered a trial run at a last meal. No matter, we savored it for the delicious moment that it was and retired to the front room of the Isaac Shelby Crouch house, where during the past 150 years there have been many funeral services and many a conversation about how they should be done, including the washing and the watching of bodies before their actual departures.

"There was a time when I thought my final resting place would be here on the farm. But, then I began to think about all the abandoned family burial places from one end of the country to the other, and finally I said, no, that won't do."

The funeral director skillfully let me do most of the talking. After all, he did have the good sense to recognize that it was, after all, *my* funeral, and I was paying for it. I also remembered that the graves of great-grandmother Cynthia and great-grandfather John were "lost" somewhere in the ages, and I had always believed they had deserved something better.

"I finally came to the realization that I ought to be buried in grandfather's (Cynthia's son) and grandmother's plot in North Middletown. That's where my mother is too and there's plenty of room there." Just across the way are the graves of my other grandparents, and my father sleeps with them. Up in the other direction, on the other side of the gentle slope are my maternal great-grandparents. My stepfather, uncles, aunts, and cousins too all wait here for the Resurrection and Final Judgment, their ultimate peaces at the center. And why not I? And why not my loved one who watches and listens from across the room, where the portrait of Cynthia hangs above the mantlepiece as I unburden my own body and soul?

"No metal casket for me," said she.

"Wood then?" said the funeral director, seeing both an opening, as well as an opportunity to break the uncomfortable silence that followed.

"Yes," said she.

"Let's make them both walnut," I replied, throwing both caution and cost to the wind.

"And don't forget the Olympia Marching Band on the return from the cemetery," she said with a smile, remembering the time I had hired the five-piece French Quarter band and had met her coming in to Moissant Airport in New Orleans from her long stay in South America. The coroner of Orleans Parish, Frank Minyard, and his four friends had played, oh, Lordy me, how they had played the sweet juice out of "When the Saints Go Marching In," and we trucked our way from the gatehouse to the main concourse, before going down to Felix's on Iberville Street to gorge ourselves with oysters on the half-shells. Oh, we were deliciously in love. What a life we had lived! And we'd show 'em how to go out in style! What marvelous Dixieland music would be heard on the return from the cemetery!

And so, now it was time to think of ringing down some curtains, and ringing in an after-life. By midnight, the plans were formed. We said our goodbyes to the funeral director and his wife, then took ourselves to our bed to love, to sleep, to dream, to live each additional, bonus day without concern, and without regret. At that moment, we spoke no more of dying, and we recalled with joy the simple living of our lives.

1906-1988

"Nobody knows how long anybody is going to live....
when you get to my age, you've got
to think about what can I do with whatever is left of it."

– Barry Bingham Sr. –

*U*pstream from Louisville, the Ohio River at Three Mile Island was broad and shimmering in the hot mid-August heat. The drive through the main gate at Glenview was a time for slowing down to take in the sound of the crickets in the thickly forested ravines. The huge, ancient trees and the wild foliage shut out the noise of the speedboats on the river and the automobiles on River Road.

The ascent to the private estate was like a staircase to exhilarating levels unexperienced by most. And yet, there was comfort in the knowledge and remembrance that Barry Bingham Sr., a giant among publishers of locally-owned, major newspapers, *The Courier-Journal* and *The Louisville Times*, was everyman's hope. (*The Times* had been merged with *The Courier-Journal* in 1987 one year after the sale of the two newspapers to the Gannett Corporation.) The walk across the expansive lawn to "The Little House" brought recollections of the elder's sons—Worth and Jonathan—who had died tragically years before the sale at the prime and most promising times of their youths. John Ed Pearce, who had written brilliantly for *The Courier-Journal* in the glory days of the Bingham family's leadership, stood outside in the blistering sun to greet old friends as they came to pay their last respects to the man who had always exemplified the finest.

Inside "The Little House," modest as only cottages can be—as if paying its own respect and deference to the family mansion, "Melcombe Bingham" across the way, where Barry Jr. and his family live—the line of mourners passed circumspectly through the room, where reposed the casket containing the body of the patriarch.

I was one among many journalists who spoke briefly to the widow, Mary Caperton Bingham, and the only surviving son, Barry Jr., expressing in words that failed to convey adequately the depth of the feeling, appreciation for the man who had served the profession of journalism so well. I had never known the Bingham daughters, "Sallie" and Eleanor, and later I would come to understand how they as females had struggled for recognition in the family's management of the newspapers.

Back on the lawn, I watched as more old friends arrived. There was a pervading silence. Only the hum and the intermittent chirping of the insects up and down the long, winding driveway broke the stillness. Both the "Melcombe Bingham" mansion and "The Little House" seemed lost in loneliness.

And such was the two-hour drive home from Louisville to Plum Lick, a time for introspection, an examination of my own life, still incomplete. My seven years as a journalist at Mr. Bingham's WHAS Radio and Television, and the following 19 years at Mr. Paley's CBS News, had been rich in satisfaction beyond all reasonable expectations of a little boy from Bourbon County, Kentucky. There had been so many brief, shining moments, all counting had been lost. To have counted would have destroyed the magic of that quarter of a century.

Down the road, the view toward the year 2000—from the School of Journalism at the University of Kentucky to the book-lined, upstairs room in the old house on Plum Lick—would owe its vitality and its validity in large measure to the patrician who had gone before. Barry Bingham Sr. was a 20th-century man for all seasons. More than that, he inspired others to reach beyond themselves, as Browning had challenged all generations to reach beyond their grasps. And so, a young and callow journalist would leave the safer security of Louisville to aspire to the heights of network news. During those 19 years—in Washington, D.C., Atlanta, Caracas, and Dallas, and in hundreds of places from Bakersfield to Boston to Beirut—the inspiration, which came down from Glenview, had never failed.

The day following the visitation, my wife and I drove again from Plum Lick to Louisville, a journey that needed to be made—could not have avoided being made—because some things simply must be done.

Calvary Episcopal Church on South Fourth Street in Louisville was filled for the "Service of Praise to God And In Thanksgiving For The Life Of Barry Bingham, February 10, 1906—August 15, 1988." Typical of his quiet generosity, his unassuming nature, the name of Barry Bingham Sr. was not uttered during the service. Instead, the organ preludes of Johann Sebastian Bach reached out to every pew and every corner of the old church. The collected voices of the Calvary Church choir and the Louisville Bach Society intoned the Brahms anthem, "How lovely is Thy Dwelling Place."

Before the procession to Cave Hill Cemetery, where swans were swimming on the lake, there was a reading from *Pilgrim's Progress:*

Then, he said, I am going to my Father's and though with great difficulty I am got hither, yet now I do not repent me of all the trouble I have been at to arrive where I am.

My sword I give to him that shall succeed me in my pilgrimage and my courage and skill to him that can get it. My marks and scars I carry with me, to be a witness for me, that I have fought his battle who now will be my rewarder.

When the day that he must go hence was come,
*   many accompanied him to the river side, into*
which as he went he said, 'Death where is thy
sting?' And as he went down deeper, he said,
'Grave where is victory?'

So he passed over, and all the trumpets sounded
for him on the other side.

Time

> "We live in deeds, not years; in thoughts, not breaths,
> In feelings, not in figures on a dial.
> We should count time by heart-throbs."
>
> **— Philip James Bailey —**

*T*ime is becoming more precious with each tick of the clock on the mantlepiece here on Plum Lick. Squandering a single minute has become no small concern. Perhaps the passage of three score years and four has acted as a messenger for Old Ben himself:

"Dost thou love life? Then do not squander time, for that's the stuff life is made of."

Ben Franklin, 15th son of a family of 17 children, started out virtually penniless. An apprentice for his older brother, James, Ben was an untypical 12-year-old. He was not only smart, but had a sure sense of how to use his talents and his time to better his condition. By the time he was only 26 years old he had begun publishing *Poor Richard's Almanac.*

"For want of a nail, the shoe was lost; for want of a shoe the horse was lost; and for want of a horse the rider was lost."

This "time" thinking is much on my mind these days. The reality is that time as we know it here on Earth is finite: it has boundaries, it is not everlasting, it is short-lived. Knowing this causes me to wonder why is there so much recklessness about how to spend such a God-given substance? It has started me to figuring.

Were I to live to be 100 years of age, it would mean on my next birthday I will have 35 more years of precious, irreplaceable life as a GIFT. It cannot be bought anywhere at any price. It cannot be requested. It is a sparkling piece of magic. It includes a presumption that I will be well in body and mind, and specifically it includes the cure of the cancer detected in my prostate in late 1993.

My days are therefore numbered (leap years mean nothing to me): 12,775—no more, no less. Old Ben might smile as I carry the calculations down to the very last tick: 306,600 hours; 18,396,000 minutes; 1,103,760,000 seconds. I know it sounds like the national debt, and it certainly would be ludicrous to be staring continuously at the clock on the mantlepiece, muttering: "Only 1,103,759,999 seconds left to live." I'm simply trying to educate myself to the fact that time is finite and irreplaceable. Infinity will begin (if my glory train arrives at the station on time) in 2,030.

If I could *"hold infinity in the palm of [my] hand,"* as Blake said, I should want to remember that there's an accompanying danger of believing that my mortal hand is forever. While I might wish to consider eternity by smelling, from time to time, a flower in summer, I should not want to delude myself by thinking I have finite time to fritter away when there is honest and important labor at hand. The challenges of trying to live a good life seem to involve a balancing of finite time with infinite possibilities. They seem to depend upon one another.

Living out 1,103,760,000 seconds selfishly would appear to be a terrible waste of time. The mind yearns for eternity, where Old Ben now resides. It is impossible to know for sure, but he and Poor Richard would probably applaud us being up and about our various vocations, while at the same time paying our respects to the even greater reality of the world to come.

Our bodies, as Ben Franklin's...will become as the *"cover of an old book, its contents worn out, and script of its lettering and gilding...will...appear once more in a new and more beautiful edition, corrected and amended by its Author."*

So, there I am standing by the mantlepiece, looking at the clock from Tiffany's given to me by CBS upon my "retirement." The inscription includes words used so often by myself throughout those 19 years when I literally lived my life by the sweep of the second hand: "Pace Yourself." The portrait of great-grandmother Cynthia looks down upon me, along with the portrait of my soul mate, Lalie, which graces the adjacent wall, and from above the mantlepiece across the hallway, Lucile, my mother, looks down from her portrait created when she was about 16 years old, a life beginning with fresh innocence, ending 58 years later, her battle with cancer over, the expression on her face at the moment of her death one of heavenly peace.

Moving smoothly through life with as much peace at the center as possible is one of the good ways of conducting the train through the stops along the way to the roundhouse. It includes attention to detail, but also time off for viewing the countryside. Balancing these two considerations becomes an important piece of business. How nice it always was to see the conductor of the train removing a gold timepiece from a well buttoned vest, considering the exact moment of the day, and knowing precisely when to exclaim with authority: "All abooooard!"

That's how I wish to feel as I stand by the mantlepiece and have the courage and the inspiration to say to myself: "It's time to live!"

Judge

"For tho' from out our bourne of Time and Place
The flood may bear me far,
I hope to see my Pilot face to face
When I have crost the bar."

– Alfred, Lord Tennyson –

*S*tanding near the coffin containing the body of Bert T. Combs, the minister read the poem by Rudyard Kipling, *If*—capturing for one stinging moment the gamble taken by the late governor on the night of December 3, 1991, a portrait of nature colliding with mankind, the words filling the church like strong, unforgiving Red River flash flood waters.

> *If you can make one heap of all your winnings*
> *And risk it on one turn of pitch-and-toss,*
> *And lose, and start again at your beginnings*
> *And never breathe a word about your loss.*

"He wanted to be home that night," said Rev. Harold Dorsey at the Manchester Baptist Church late on the morning of December 7. Bert Combs, 80 years old, had risked everything, and he had lost. Or, had he really lost? Had he not ascended, achieved, and earned his peace at the center? Had he not gone out on the high tide, when he had tried to cross the floodwaters and had been swept away by them?

"He wanted to be home that night," echoed like an anthem on the long, twisting drive from the church to the cemetery on Beech Creek in Clay County. The words of James Still's *Heritage*, too, were a part of the music of a lifetime begun and ended in the mountains of eastern Kentucky. The former governor's favorite lines of poetry had been read at the Capitol rotunda in Frankfort, where he had lain in state on December 6, 1991, and again at the church in Manchester, and they were framed and hung on the wall of the dining room at Fern Hill.

> *I shall not leave these prisoning hills*
> *Though they topple their barren heads to level earth...*
> *And one with death rising to bloom again, I cannot go.*
> *Being of these hills I cannot pass beyond.*

The hills of his native Eastern Kentucky that the Governor loved so well were on that early Saturday afternoon imprisoning a long line of cars following the hearse, winding miles deep into the Clay County watershed of the Red Bird River. To some, it may have seemed desolate. To others, it may have appeared rough and impoverished. To the family and friends of "Judge" it was a necessary passage through time, a going back to roots as natural and as simple as the mournful baying of a hound on the hill, crows calling from ridge to ridge, the busy clucking of chickens in the backyards of modest homes, the sounds of good people preparing for the coming of another winter.

"Judge" was a name he had heard as often as "Governor" in his later years, especially by Sara, his soul mate, who forever after would mean one thing and one thing only whenever she uttered the single, simple word "Judge."

It was a right smart climb up the side of the hill, where the Beech Creek Cemetery looks out over the valley bearing the waters of the Red Bird to the South Fork of the Kentucky, later joined by the Red onward through the Gorge and the Palisades to the Capitol in Frankfort. The honorary pallbearers were eight former governors— Lawrence Wetherby, Ned Breathitt, Louis Nunn, Julian Carroll, Wendell Ford, John Y. Brown Jr., Martha Layne Collins and Wallace Wilkinson; former Lt. Gov. Wilson Wyatt; and newly-elected Gov. Brereton Jones.

Judge had come home to be laid to rest beside Stephen, his father, and Martha, his mother. The inspiration, love, and commitment of

Martha Jones Combs had been remembered by Reverend Dorsey in the Manchester Baptist Church. "A man called from the hills" to make a difference throughout the Commonwealth was to become the meaning of the life of Martha's son, Bert. And this would be the day that he, Sara, their family, and friends would be lifting their eyes unto the hills. For as the mountain poet, James Still, wrote beautifully and well in Heritage: *"I cannot leave, I cannot go away."*

When the graveside services were near their end, Reverend Dorsey announced the tradition of Beech Creek Cemetery, the singing of "Amazing Grace", and Tommy, Judge's son, who, despite the difficulty of his mental impediment, thinking perhaps the old song might *not* be sung, said loudly: "And I'm gong to sing it, by God."

It was more than most voices could bear, but the words of the fine old hymn resounded in the hills, and it was good. The friend from Plum Lick went to speak to Sara, Judge Combs' young, intelligent, deeply caring widow. They talked about the farm in Powell County, where Judge was returning the night he died.

"I'm going to keep the farm," she said. "He would have wanted it that way."

Sara's words were reassuring at a time when so many were continuing to abandon farms for urban conveniences; she would feel the need of staying on the land despite almost immediate advice from friends that she should sell Fern Hill and move back to Louisville, the place where she was born and had grown up as a city girl. It was plain to see she had no intention of heeding the advice, not even from well-meaning friends.

"You'll have to come and visit, so we can compare notes. Our farm sounds a lot like your farm," she said to me, and her words, filled with love and hope, were a real and certain comfort on the drive home from the hills of Clay County to the lowlands of Bourbon and the valley of Plum Lick.

Sara

"When you are old and grey and full of sleep,
And nodding by the fire, take down this book,
And slowly read, and dream of the soft look
Your eyes had once, and of their shadows deep;

"...And bending down beside the glowing bars,
Murmur, a little sadly, how Love fled
And paced upon the mountains overhead
And hid his face amid a crowd of stars."

– William Butler Yeats –

*T*wo years and four months went by. Sara had become a judge in her own time, and most would agree, by her own abilities. She, as well as Judge, had been valedictorians in their respective high schools and colleges, salutatorians in their law schools. She had been appointed by Governor Brereton Jones on July 17, 1993, to become the first woman to serve on the Kentucky State Supreme Court, and she served until November 19th of that year, following her narrow defeat by Janet Stumbo in the regular election on November 2.

After the defeat, Sara did not leave the cabin at Fern Hill for ten days. She was frustrated, embarrassed, and sorely disappointed. When she finally emerged, she went quickly to work to re-establish her private law practice in Powell County, believing that it was the only way she'd stand any chance of holding on to the one thing Judge had left her in his will—the farm at Fern Hill. Once again, she received an appointment from Governor Jones. This time, he named her to the Seventh District Court of Appeals, representing 22 Eastern Kentucky counties, the seat which had been vacated by Janet Stumbo. Sara closed her law office in Stanton, and in 1994 she was running for election again. Ironically, her husband had begun his political career as an appointee by Gov. Lawrence Wetherby to the Court of Appeals of Kentucky, the highest court in the state in 1951, the same seat to which Sara had been appointed 42 years later. It was where he'd begun his political career. It was where she was hoping for her own new beginning.

Sara was waiting at the door of her home at Fern Hill on a rainy Sunday afternoon, April 3, 1994. There was an infectious beaming on her face, a smile that seemed to extend to the soles of her tiny feet. Hilda Mae, the St. Bernard, roared, serving notice that what stood between her and Sara Combs was a whole lot of tooth. There were Rusty Red Dog, the golden retriever who went everywhere that Sara went, and Woolfie, the inside dog but a consummate chaser of cars when given the opportunity, and the younger Sophie, an outside dog, who had not yet ventured to taste the wild joys of car-chasing. The four dogs competed for tail-wagging rights, while Trash, the cat, recently declawed, substantially paranoid about roguish dogs, was manipulating the opening of cabinets with muted paws. Callie, the less reckless of the cats, moved stealthily in the time-honored tradition of all cats.

Inside the vaulted living room, the portrait of Judge hung near the huge fireplace, where he and Sara had married on December 30, 1988. He had seemed fidgety on that day, awkwardly shy in his formal attire, but in the easygoing portrait of him, in his flannel shirt and cream-colored bush jacket, the soft smile seemed to follow visitors wherever they went. They knew he was still there.

On the facing wall was Dylan Thomas' "Fern Hill," a poem of love and greenness and strength, the definition for Judge's and Sara's carving out of their farm on Lower Cane Creek Road on 200 acres from a hilltop to a hilltop in the heartland of Powell County. From this poem had come the name, "Fern Hill." "...*It was all shining, it was Adam and maiden...*"

The original plan for the rose garden lay near the desk where

Judge had sat and looked through the front window, where he had witnessed the ripening of the seasons up and down Lower Cane Creek. The words on the paper were in Judge's own handwriting, saved by Sara, who was committed now to perpetuating the memory of the man from the mountains who had been Kentucky's governor in the first half of the difficult decade of the 1960s, the man who had signed the executive order forbidding racial discrimination in public accommodations, the man from Prestonsburg, whose twang was past helping by experts of elocution. Judge's speech was so "bad" it was credited with helping him to emerge victorious in his second attempt to be elected Governor of Kentucky. A lover of flowers, Judge had created during his administration the giant floral clock in Frankfort, which his political enemy "Happy" Chandler could not resist ridiculing: "They don't say it's half past two in Frankfort, they say it's two petunias past the jimsonweed."

Governor from 1959 to 1963, Combs served from 1967 to 1970 on the Federal Court of Appeals, where the name "Judge" permanently attached itself, but he left the bench in Cincinnati, Sara said, because he was not content. He ran for governor again in 1971, but he lost to Wendell Ford. Then, Judge established the prestigious law firm, Wyatt, Tarrant and Combs in Louisville. It was there he met Sara. She was studying law, and she became his law clerk.

In time, she became the keeper of his heart.

On Easter Day in 1994, the sun was hidden behind scudding clouds at Fern Hill. The rain fell intermittently, and the wind played the chimes on the long back porch facing the western hill covered with budding trees that in the distance gave the impression that the earth was emitting puffs of pale green Maple smoke. The occasional sharp crack of lightning and its thunder rolling up and down the valley served as rueful reminder of the night more than two years before, when Judge was lost and Sara had sought in vain through the night and parts of the next day to find him.

"He went out on high tide," said Sara, as she recalled the cold, wet night, December 3, 1991, when the wall of brown, dirty, swirling water of the Red River roared out of Daniel Boone National Forest, sweeping through the valley where the roads and the paths and the frailties of mankind are no match for nature's upheavals, retchings to destroy, yet at the same time providing for a cleansing of the earth. The stubble of the cornfield along the banks of the Red River where Judge died was a hushed reminder that humans share a commonality with crops and trees no matter how deeply rooted.

"He didn't drown," said Sara. "When they found him, they had a difficult time loosening the grip he had on the limb," a part of the bush he had seized on the bank of the main channel on the edge of the flood plain. He had died of hypothermia, low body temperature, and in Judge's case, fatally low.

He had been past the low place in the road many times when the tide was rolling down, and many was the time he had forded the rising waters, but this time he miscalculated. The front wheels of the car entered the stream, and water quickly lapped higher above the front bumper and around the bottom frames of the doors. The engine drowned out. There was an insistent, muffled pounding of the rising current. Judge probably opened the door while there still was time, and he stepped out into the flooded roadway. He likely thought he would walk away to high ground. A sudden flash of water had lifted the big Lincoln sedan, with Judge's briefcase inside, and swept it into the ditch.

Judge probably lost his footing; he might have been thrown off balance. Whatever happened, he too was swept away and carried downstream. Instinctively, he removed his shoes, then his trousers and his heavy winter clothing. He tried to swim. But a man half Judge's age could not match the current. He was floundering. The windchill was about 20 below zero. Judge might have lived two minutes as he struggled to stay afloat, hoping to be spilled upon some dry place.

In those two minutes, bits and pieces of 80 years of vibrancy and brilliance born in and of the Eastern Kentucky mountains likely flashed through Judge's consciousness like stars collapsing from their constellations, like the beating down of thunder and the crash of lightning into the treetops pointed upward and outward, always reaching higher.

Judge might have thought he had found a single piece of dry earth in the small limb to which he held with all the physical strength that was left in him. He may have called out the name "Jibbo," his favorite name for Sara. He may not have had time to call for help as he was carried downstream a distance of a half-mile, passing beneath the four-lane highway named in his honor, the Bert T. Combs Mountain Parkway, conceived and completed during his administration as Governor of the Commonwealth. But, if he did call out in the darkness, there would be no answer from the cars with windows tightly rolled up, speeding back and forth, spewing water in all directions on the parkway from Prestonsburg to Winchester, some drivers cursing the night, while below in the river the man from the mountains was experiencing the hypothermia sensation—the cold that turns to warmth, the euphoria of approaching sleep, the delusion of safety—then the passing over from this life to the next.

"I see car lights down there," a woman in a nearby house said to her husband.

"Aw, you don't see anything," the man replied, and they went to bed and soon were asleep.

On the morning and early afternoon of April 3, 1994, Sara had been to visit with Judge's sister, Louise Marcum, in Manchester, stopping for a while at the Baptist Church there, then making the annual pilgrimage to stand at Judge's grave at Beech Creek Cemetery, to place a lily there for him because Easter was always his favorite day of their brief lives together. Although 37 years had separated them in age, and Sara had been Judge's third wife, he her third husband, age was not a barrier to the joy they had come to know. It was a confirmation that love transcends chronological conventions.

Judge had given Sara an orchid or rose corsage to wear each Easter and she had saved all of them in their individual boxes, each now reposing, crumbling with the passage of the years, fragrances blowing drier, withering on the basement shelves at Fern Hill. The shelves also held jars of preserved food grown by Judge's own hand in the garden he tended in the 80th and final year of his life.

Judge always called Sara, "Pee Jib" or "Jib" or "Jibbo." In the eastern Kentucky mountains, the pee jib is the small, powerful "taw," the marble used to strike with thumb and first finger the other marbles in the circle of the game of "keeps." Sara always called her lover, friend, and husband, "Judge," not "Governor."

"We have carved something beautiful out of the wilderness, haven't we, Jibbo?" Judge said to Sara as they walked up to the cabin on the afternoon of December 2, 1991.

"We'll make it more beautiful with each passing year, Judge," said the woman from the big city of Louisville, replying in the softness of her love for the man from the mountains, who at that moment had but one day to live.

The rains kept coming and had been for days. A Rockcastle woman had been swept away by the flood. The runoff of water from the hill to the rear of the cabin had begun to flood the basement at Fern Hill.

"We are in for a terrible siege, Judge. Let's go in and stay up as late as we can and keep vigil over the house."

Early dawn Tuesday, December 3, 1991, Judge talked with his

daughter, Lois, by telephone. To Jibbo, he seemed at peace. She had a 2 p.m. court date in Louisville for the settlement of her father's estate, and Judge had work to do in Lexington. He was organizing a fund-raising gala for the newly-elected governor, Brereton Jones.

"Jibbo, Honey, I will get home ahead of you tonight. I'll start supper, and we'll either have chicken or fish. I'll make you a big pot of bean soup. I'll build you a fire, and I'll pour you a good drink. You wait and see, Honey. You'll feel better when you get home to me tonight."

"Thank you, Sweetheart. I always feel better when I get home to you, and I'll especially need you tonight."

Sara finished her legal work in Louisville. It was about 7:30 p.m., December 3, when she placed the first call to tell Judge she was heading east from the city on Interstate 64. She called Lexington and Fern Hill, but there was no answer. She could not know that approximately the same time she was calling Judge, he was approaching the low place in the road between Stanton and Fern Hill.

He had decided to try to cross the water where the road dips down at a place where it looks as if a giant hand has reached in and scooped out the earth, and Judge didn't see any reason why he couldn't cross it because he had done it so many times before during both winter and spring floods.

It was bitterly cold.

Sara tried to call again at 8:45 p.m., but there was still no answer. She began to be more seriously worried. She had pulled off the interstate at one of the Shelbyville exits, then again at Frankfort, at Lexington, and at Winchester, each mile marker where she knew she could quickly find a telephone. She had made telephone calls from the 28-mile marker at 8:00, the 35-mile marker at 8:10, and she had made calls from the public telephones at the 48-, 55-, and 94-mile markers on Interstate 64.

It was not like Judge to cause her to worry like this, and his last words to her had begun to haunt her:

"Jibbo, Honey, I'll get home ahead of you tonight."

Rusty, Sara's faithful Rusty Red Dog, slept fitfully on the front seat of the small car. He was a sensitive animal, seeming to understand things well beyond his natural inability to comprehend as a human would. Each time she stopped to make a telephone call, Rusty's disquietude deepened.

Judge had finished his work on Governor Jones' fund-raising gala after working on it most of the afternoon. He had stopped by his condominium in Lexington, as he frequently did, had poured himself a Scotch, and in checking his watch might have remembered what he had told Jibbo:

"I'll start supper...I'll make you a big pot of bean soup...I'll build you a fire...."

Judge was last seen going down on an elevator in Lexington about 5:30 p.m. After the stop at the condominium, he had left the garage door open, later causing State Trooper Ernie Dudleson to ask Sara if there were any reason to believe that there might have been foul play? She had not been able to think of any. Ernie was a professional, and he would ask the difficult question: might there have been another woman? Sara wished there could have been—she was frantically wishing any reason for the absence other than the danger she feared had befallen him.

Judge must have left Lexington about 6:30. He probably was in Stanton and on the road to Fern Hill about 7:45. Later, that would be established as approximately the time he disappeared into the flood waters.

At 9:20 p.m. there were still only constant rings on the phone each time Sara stopped to call. After the Winchester exit, when it was 9:45, she was in a panic. She kept looking for skid marks on the interstate, thinking he might have gone to sleep at the wheel, might have driven off the road. She turned onto the Mountain Parkway, raced down it, thinking no longer of telephones, wanting only to reach Fern Hill. At Exit 22 at Stanton she took "the long way."

The long way meant she would not have to cross the low place in the road where Judge had miscalculated, but the long way would take her near the edge of the bend in the river where at that moment Judge held in the powerful grip of death the limb on the bank of the river. But she could not look down and see him. It would have been virtually impossible for her to have done that. She would see reflected in the headlights of her car only the sweep of brown, churning water as it spread wider in the valley.

"I passed him many times during the night as he floated in that swollen river," Sara said of her frantic search for any sign of Judge.

The darkness was total.

"Please, God, let him be alive," was all Sara could think. "Please God, let me get to him in time. God, don't let him be gone."

She turned onto Lower Cane Creek Road and sped to the little wooden bridge at the entrance to Fern Hill. She had prayed that maybe the gate would be unlocked, the one, last desperate hope seen as a sign that Judge was home after all, that he had been out to check on the miniature horses at the barn and had left the gate open for her.

It was locked.

"My God, he's dead!" Sara screamed to Rusty.

She opened the gate and drove up the hill to the cabin. She was alone, except for Rusty, thank God for him, but by now Rusty was confused and fearful that something dreadful had taken place. He lay on the floor, head down, eyes deeply troubled, as Sara placed calls to Judge's daughter to ask if she'd heard from him. Wouldn't it have been an embarrassment if Sara had called State Police prematurely? The question had been asked, but she would wait no longer. At five minutes before 11, Sara called Trooper Dwight O'Hair in Stanton. Failing to reach him, she then called the Kentucky State Police Headquarters in Morehead. She reported that she thought something terrible had happened.

Trooper Ernie Dudleson was sent to Fern Hill. Before he arrived, Sara was pacing the floor. Shock was creeping over her. It was then she was sure she heard a voice—a voice filled with great joy.

"Hello, Jib, where are you?"

It was Judge calling from the back door!

"It's him! He's home!" Sara cried, and she ran to meet him, but when she opened the door and looked outside, it was dark. There was no one there. Only the darkness. She returned inside and waited.

The lights of Trooper Dudleson's cruiser appeared at the gate. He drove to the cabin, entered, and in a few minutes he and Sara were talking about what might have occurred. There were no clues. Judge could have gone to sleep while driving. He could have had a heart attack. And, yes, there was the flash flood.

"Would you like to come along while I search?" asked the tall, slender trooper with the softness of voice that comes from being a mountain man.

"Oh, yes, please take me along...I will be very quiet, but please let me go."

Trooper Dudleson suggested that Sara leave a note on the door in the event that Judge might return. And, after all, he should have a way of knowing that others were concerned about him, shouldn't he? It was Ernie Dudleson's way of comforting Sara, giving her a small piece of hope, when he instinctively knew it was probably without basis, and the note was still on the door where Sara had left it when Dudleson and she returned the next morning after retracing Judge's probable route from Lexington to Powell County.

"Judge—
Am out looking for you with KSP. Will be back soon.
Love."

They had not found a sign of him. As they looked out over the low place in the road where Judge had first entered the water, Ernie asked

Sara if she thought he might have tried to cross there?

"Yes," she replied.

Trooper Dudleson knew then, that if Judge had tried to cross, and if he had been swept away, it would be very unlikely that any trace of him would ever be found. It had happened so many times before to victims of flash floods in the mountains of Kentucky, bodies lost amid debris as it swirled its way through the Kentucky River, the Ohio, and the Mississippi Rivers to the Gulf of Mexico.

Oh, yes, some of Judge's critics would ask, wasn't it ironic that the manhandling of the mountain earth by the coal mining industry, which Judge had over a period of 10 years defended in court, would in time wreak its vengeance upon him in the river?

Reminded of this in the summer of 1994, Sara replied: "The do-gooders who successfully blocked the building of the Red River Gorge Dam" also share in the blame for the annual flooding that continues to be so deadly destructive.

About 8 a.m. on December 4, Judge's car was found against a large tree in about five feet of water approximately 400 feet from the road. Judge's body was found downstream about noon the same day.

At ten minutes to one, Sara was told.

She would say, two-and-a-half years later in the spring of 1994, after looking for the first time at a picture that had been taken when he was found on the bank of the river, that Judge looked as if he were in a baptismal font with a look of total peace on his face.

On Memorial Day weekend, the hummingbirds return to Fern Hill, sometimes 30 to 40 of them. On the third week in February, the bluebirds arrive to begin cleaning out the fence row. The frogs begin their chirping sounds on March 11; and by May 15, they have grown into croakers. The sweet fragrance of the Star Magnolia is in bloom, preceding the Dogwood blossoms in the third week of April. A lone male Kentucky cardinal sees his own reflection in the windows of the cabin, and he attacks furiously, striking his beak and flailing his blood-bright body against the glass to scare away the offender and to demonstrate to his mate perched close by that he really docs care. The red-wing blackbirds fly back and forth over Lower Cane Creek where it flows, dividing Fern Hill into two parts. In the back of the cabin, where normally a rivulet of crystal water descends the ravine, Judge and Jibbo had placed a bench for sitting, for talking, or for quiet reflection. There's a statue of St. Francis of Assisi, symbol of hope for the smallest of creatures, standing watch over the graceful peace of Fern Hill, cloaking all who pass that way.

On the following Sunday, I sat with Sara near the kitchen in the cabin, and I recorded our conversation. There was a problem with the tape recorder, and it was necessary to start over again, and so I shared with Sara the first notes I'd taken.

DAVID:
Let me tell you what I've written down so far: a sense of integrity; more than that, a sense of honor; "integer;" a wholeness; a stage where one has to pull together experiences, lessons, and bring them all together; grab all concepts and feelings and have cohesive meaning.
SARA:
Oh, Lord, I've said too much, haven't I? And I'm rambling. Well, I really, uh,—Woolfie, quit that!—I went back to your discussion of it

last night when you used the word integrity—I thought that was a very good beginning for *Peace at the Center*. When I think of integrity, I think of it as more than just the sense of honor to which we all value and aspire, a sort of Cyrano de Bergerac sense of honor. But, it's more than that. It goes back to the Latin root "integer," which meant wholeness. We even use that in mathematics—a whole number is an integer, not a fraction but a complete number in and of itself.

I believe that one doesn't arrive at that philosophical and mathematical purity until having undergone many life experiences. Now, I think it arrives in a person in different stages, maybe based on one's training and experience and background. My concept of it is simply this: whatever values, training, philosophy, even religion one has learned in the course of a life, the childhood values from the cradle, through adolescence, through college, are all there.

They are all part of the person, but not until one undergoes the crucible, perhaps, puts all those values to the test in the crucible of life experience—you know—a great love, a great passion, and, I think, a great sorrow. I think one has to suffer before all these values can be tested. No doubt, we can select what's necessary for our survival and then go on and arrive at a kind of ability to deal with one's self as a whole person. Then, turn outward after you grab all this in from the outer universe into yourself and come to terms with what it will take for one to cope and survive with a sense of one's own honor and integrity. Then one starts to deal differently with the world, and that's your peace at the center.

That's where you, I think, handle the world from your *own* perspective instead of reacting to the world in order to form that perspective.

DAVID:

Can you go beyond what you describe as Judge's "accident," his 'going out on high tide,' and relate it to eternity?

SARA:

I think what it does is give us our sense of where we are in the eternal scheme of things, and it's both a very grand and a very humbling concept all at the same time. I think we learn how very insignificant our space on this earth is in terms of the chronology involved and yet how very precious that short chronology is because it is so short.

The term is "ephemeral". In *The Little Prince*, which is one of my favorite works, Antoine de Saint-Exupéry describes the word, "éphémère," it is from the Greek word "ephemeris," we call it "ephemeral", it's translated that way. The Little Prince asks the rose, who is his foil in the story, almost a parable, why is the rose so precious? Because it is ephemeral. What does that mean? It means that it is subject to rapid change, and therefore that which is subject to rapid change becomes yet more precious because it's likely to elude us at any given time, and we know not what time and in what fashion. That's sort of the drama and the tragedy of life, all in one.

(The sounds of thunder rolled repeatedly across the Lower Cane Creek hills, and the accompanying bolts of lightning cracked nearby, making it seem as if a massive metaphor of storms had been planned by a power greater than humans could change or comprehend.)

That's why I think that a tragedy teaches us more maybe even than a great love, because it reinforces that notion of the ephemeral nature or the elusive nature of what we love. We best be making the most of it at all times. We best be following our hearts and finding out what's important to us and not be wasting a lot of time because we also are ephemeral. We are subject to rapid change and disappearance just as those things are that we love and we seek to possess.

DAVID:

You have also mentioned the importance of letting go. What do you mean by that?

SARA:

I mean that when that which we love most, whether it be a person, a position, an ambition, whatever it is that people love the most, and I prefer the person aspect of it, I prefer a great love in my life over ambition or anything else, it just means more to me. But when that loss occurs, I think what the grieving process essentially means is we are either able to let go of it or we perish. It teaches you to let go of everything in life that you can't control.

You know everything is lent to us for a while, nothing is given; and when it's time to be reclaimed, if we don't let go of it we either look greedy and grabby and stupid, because we can't hold it back, or we destroy ourselves in the process. And if you do let go, there comes a kind of grace and a kind of peace and an ability to accept what comes next. If we don't let go of that which we've lost, then we're never open to accept whatever comes along again.

DAVID:

Did you and Judge talk about it, in this way?

SARA:

No, not really. He thought that he had more time, and I thought he had more time. But that last summer—and I may have mentioned this, I can't remember what I've put in that section of my book manuscript you read—that last summer I don't know if I had a premonition of what was to come, or whether my natural worrying tendencies just took hold of me. I worried about him constantly, and if he got a hangnail, I worried about him. Finally, you know, one day he stayed home from the office and worked in the garden and we had lunch here, and we were standing right over here in the kitchen, having a drink before lunch, and I started this worrying, and I said, "Judge, I just don't know what I'd do without you. How could I ever live without you?"

"You have got to quit this worrying," he said. "You are agonizing over the future and destroying the present in the process. Absent a tragedy," he said, and these were his very words, "I believe we have another ten years together."

You know, the way he said it, he didn't say, "I have another ten years to live." He said, "I *believe* we have another ten years." And I think he contemplated that he would have vigorous and healthy and good time left to him because he was so healthy. He was in his prime at eighty years old; he was like a very vigorous and young fifty. He was blessed with tremendous health, and his intellect was as keen as ever—if not keener. He had felt peace at the center, I think, at long last. It came to him fairly late in life. He'd always been philosophical. He'd always been, I guess, almost Spartan in his approach to life. Very Stoic, definitely Stoic would be the word for it, to the point of being fatalistic. He expected the worst to happen to him because most of his life it had. When something wonderful happened like this, it took him a while to come to terms with it, to believe it, and to have peace at the center. He had been very unhappy in his personal life, I think, most of his life.

DAVID:

How do you see the future at Fern Hill?

SARA:

Well, I don't know if I see the future, or hope for the future. I hope to be able to maintain it—not just the way he left it but to constantly be improving it in little ways, in the ways we would have improved it had he lived: never to make it gaudy or cluttered. He didn't like clutter. I'd like to be able to maintain it physically as a comfortable place to welcome people and entertain; and the main thing I want to maintain about it is the *sense* of it, the aura of his presence here, the times we spent here.

I want to have people here that are interesting and full of life, and I want to be able to talk about him and the ideas that he loved.

He loved ideas. You know, really they say there's a way we break people down: those who talk about things, those who talk about people, and those who talk about ideas—and Judge definitely talked about ideas. He was not materialistic. He didn't care about things. He wasn't a gossipy politico by any means. He only cared about talking about personalities insofar as they had an impact on the leadership and how that leadership had an impact on the direction that the state was going to take.

DAVID:

How would you describe the idea he had for Kentucky?

SARA:

The idea he had for Kentucky was that it should quit apologizing for itself, especially Eastern Kentucky. It should never be ashamed. He used to always say that he never wanted to hear young people from Eastern Kentucky apologize for being from Eastern Kentucky— that they could do anything—that the key to it was education, and that if they could get an education, they could go anywhere in this country and do anything; that what we had to do in this state was to quit consuming our seed corn and to lay back for the future, to invest in our young people.

He had a vision of education and technology, I think, that was beyond his years, and he had had that all of his life. He saw years before the FAX became popular that one could practice law in a tiny community like this and practice an international law practice anywhere in the world with technology. He hated technology actually, but he understood that it was a very powerful tool.

So his vision for Kentucky was to make it a better place and to never quit, never give up, to take the leap forward that was necessary to bite the bullet to make the investment in our infrastructure—the state parks system, the highway system—but first and foremost, ahead of the infrastructure was the investment in the human personality and intellect. Educating our people. I used to give him some quotations that he used in some of his speeches—especially during the school reform. "After bread, education is the first need of the people." He loved it!

There was another one, a Chinese proverb, that he used a lot, which basically goes this way, "If you're planning for a year, sow rice. If you're planning for a decade, plant trees. If you're planning for a lifetime, educate a child." And he really believed in that. He believed in the tremendous resource of the human intellect—the spirit—I think, simply because of the lesson of his own life—you know, reaching out for all those life experiences and drawing them to the center and then being able to relate from that inner core to the rest of the world.

He got it from his mother. Quite simply, his mother was the greatest influence on his life. She dragged him out of the pool halls of Manchester and made him go to school. And he never wanted to disappoint her. I don't know if he did it for himself as much as he did it for her; but once he did it, he saw what it did to his life and what it could do for everybody else.

DAVID:

I suppose in the short time that I have known you, I would be disappointed if you were only his curator. I'm wondering if it were not possible for his idea to be your idea, and you keep it alive and you even implement it, using the political, the judicial—all the abilities that you have.

SARA:

You know, I would like to do that, David. I think the only way that I can really keep him alive is to do his work that way in my own way. Obviously I am my own person, but I take pride in the fact that I shared so much with him and that he taught me so much. We taught each other. Really, maybe the only way that a person lives is within memory. And the best way you can perpetuate that memory is to keep their works alive. So, you talk about the political process—we talked about this a little bit last night—I came along I guess with a sense of a political awareness at the time that John Kennedy was running for office and he was quoting Aristotle and he was quoting, I guess one of the sections that—what was it? I can't remember now, it wasn't the *Poetics*, but he had a speech about the notion of a democracy. What is a democracy, basically? And in it he essentially said that politics is indeed the noblest profession. Public service should be considered the noblest profession, and no one is fit to live in a democracy unless he partakes of that process and contributes to it. Well, you know, it's become so corrupted; it has such a dirty image. It's not the fault of the political process. It is the result of the unfaithful stewards who've served it, and I really mean that in the true biblical sense. It is a terrible thing to be an unfaithful steward to something sacred that's entrusted to you.

Now see, Judge, I think, was a very good steward. He took over the reins of this commonwealth at a time in his life when he made up his mind he'd only be governor once very likely. Once he got there, he was going to cut a wide swath and clean up some things and drag Kentucky kicking and screaming into the 20th century. Right now, really, indeed with some of the things he did in the last part of his life, he proceeded into the 21st century. So, he knew how to use that political process the way a surgeon can use a fine tool and perform delicate surgery and do it well.

He wasn't afraid of the process. He was up to the task, and he was never corrupted by it. He loved to quote Thomas Jefferson in that he came out of office no richer than the day he entered it, materially speaking, and that was really true. He took his experience with him, with which he enriched himself. And that was essentially it. So, taking that concept, that it can be a noble profession, and that if one has something to give, it's the only arena in which you can make a difference on a very large scale other, I think, than teaching. I think that teaching and politics are the same noble calling. One just has maybe a broader base and is scrutinized more by the media.

Therein lies the rub. The reason why I would hesitate and would shrink from it all really is the media and what they've done to me personally and what I've seen them do to other people. I think that they doubt my motives, that they doubt anyone's motives. And often people live down to the lowest expectations.

DAVID:

Shouldn't they question your motives? Question them fairly? That's legitimate.

SARA:

I guess so. I think if you look at what has happened to the political process now—a political figure is accountable for every act of every assistant and every aide and every appointee and suddenly becomes not only responsible for having put that person in office, but having a sort of overall accountability for whatever that person may do in that office. Whatever wrongdoing they commit in the political process suddenly becomes attributable to the person who is the focus of the media at that point. I think there has to be a more fair approach to it all.

What if I were governor of this state and I had a corrupt cabinet secretary? I would end up being held personally accountable and ruining my family's name and my husband's name for an alleged act of corruption that may or may not have occurred but that's considered an indictable offense in a headline.

I think that the press has deviated from its role of truth-finder to creating its own version of the truth regardless of what the facts may indicate. And I think that's the tragedy of the media at present. It's a very potent tool that could be used very well to safeguard the political process. I think it's done more to corrupt the political process than some of the bad stewards who've been there because it has ultimate power. It's not accountable to anyone—only to itself.

And you know the old saying from Saint Just (executed by guillotine 200 years ago) in the French Revolution: power corrupts and absolute power corrupts absolutely. And I think that the absolute power of the press has absolutely corrupted its ability to use it well, and I think it's a tragedy. I don't say that as an indictment. I almost say it as a challenge—that it's time for real journalists who have that sense of what the art and what the craft should be about to come to the fore again and restore peace at the center of your craft the same way I think that our political leaders have to restore a sense of true integrity and honor to this political process. And I think we're going to have to work together to do it.

I don't think we can be cynical and say, "It can't be done; we've gone too far." It's not going to be done unless people start. And Judge used to always say, he said the fault of Kentucky—and you can just extrapolate it to the nation as a whole from the microcosm of this state—the fault of Kentucky is not that of the people, or the vision of the people. It's the failure of the leadership. Now I think that that leadership really is two-fold. It's the public servants who occupy the office and it's the members of the media who critique that office. Unless they come together and try to work together to elevate the sights of the people and their expectations of their leadership and their performance, we're going to become mired in a kind of hopeless cynicism that will be destructive ultimately.

DAVID:

Let me ask you a very mean, even insulting question, and I do so because it has been asked by others: how do you respond to the criticism that you were a young opportunist who took advantage of someone with the stature of Governor Bert T. Combs and you knew pretty much what the outcome would be: namely that he would not be able to outlive you. And now here you are standing in a place, a political place, a judicial place—and you didn't earn it?

SARA:

I don't know if one ever earns anything good that happens in one's life. Judge used to describe the fact he got into politics and that he became governor of this state, in the terms that he was a political accident. I'd say I'm equally a political accident. The fact that I'm here is a spinoff of our fate, really. It has to go back to how we came together—all of it. And we came together for all the right reasons. We *really* loved each other, and the only way I can talk about what is "opportunism"—I think that is one of the ugliest words in the English language. It means the using of a person in order to achieve an end and I don't think there's anything more disgraceful that one can do to a person than to use him.

DAVID:

Probably, Judge, of all people, would have spotted an opportunist...

SARA:

I think so.

DAVID:

...and nailed that person.

SARA:

I think so. I think it's one of the reasons it took him ten years to decide that all of this was for real. You know, talk is cheap and time usually ferrets out the truth about people sooner or later. We spent a lot of time together. We spent very hard times together. We had life and death experiences together during those ten years. Both of my parents died in that period of time. He nearly died—I won't say nearly died, but he had a life-threatening surgery for an abdominal aneurysm. Some of his best and closest friends died during that period of time.

Finally, after our ten years together, we had built this place and had engaged in legal battles, political battles together, and we'd achieved a kind of peace. I really was quite contented with him. Never would have changed our status unless he wanted to. He was a person who had been greatly disappointed in his life—his personal life. I didn't want for him to feel that he had to do something to please me in order to keep me. He knew that I was going to stay with him regardless of whether we married. I guess that spoke the loudest of all. You know he lived with me. I wasn't pressuring him or nagging him: "you either marry me or I will leave you;" "you either change things or I will leave you;" "you set aside a sum to take care of me or I will not marry you." It was quite the opposite. I suggested that he have a prenuptial agreement to put his children's minds to rest that he would not be marrying me to provide for me or to deprive them of their rightful inheritance, but that we would spend whatever years, if we married, together.

Once he decided he wanted to, once he decided he wanted to marry me, *I* suggested the prenuptial agreement. I believed that it enabled him to lay his own mind to rest on the subject. I was not an opportunist, certainly materially. You can ask his children when the will was read and it was determined that I was to have Fern Hill and the responsibility of it as well, not a peep was uttered that I would challenge his wishes in any way. Now, talk is cheap, but behavior speaks a lot louder. If people think that I'm a political opportunist, that's too bad. I don't care what people think [chuckle]. I haven't cared all my life...I don't know why I should start caring now. And time will test me the same way.

DAVID:

Let's get back to journalism and, maybe, breakfast can wait

because everybody else is asleep.

SARA:

(Chuckle) I'll start cooking.

DAVID:

Give me some one-word characterizations of journalism today: arrogant?

SARA:

Cynical. Witch-hunting.

DAVID:

Is that...

SARA:

Totally negative. Wholly negative. Sensational. Irresponsible, which I think is the worst. Manipulative. Opposite of what it should be: a careful, meticulous fact-finder, a ferreter-out of the truth. And then comes the duty of the editorial board to weigh the truth of the facts discovered by the dedicated reporter and to determine how that conduct should be evaluated in terms of our social philosophy.

DAVID:

Would it be accurate to say that you believe that journalists should have better *legal* minds?

SARA:

No, I think they should have better morals. I think they should go back to what their mission in society is and examine what ethical duties they have. You know, with great power comes great responsibility. They should be trained ethically, and I don't mean a code of ethics. I mean from the heart. It has to be almost a vocation—like a teacher—to take the minds over which one has control and handle that power very carefully. Not to misuse it. Not to become the Grand Inquisitor, but to mold minds very carefully, making sure that one has told the truth. But, you don't abuse. It amounts...it almost amounts to an abuse of a sacred trust. Fiduciary duty almost. To wield that power very carefully and responsibly and not to manipulate the facts.

DAVID:

Why do you think this is happening?

SARA:

Because I think it sells. It's successful. It's the quick sell. The quick thrill. The cheap thrill. Throw the people a sop that'll entertain them and they'll move on to the next cheap thrill. Instead of saying we have a mission to elevate these people, we have a mission to tell them the truth and to mold their thinking on these critical issues that will mold our society, not to provide them with one cheap thrill after another, one sensational story.

You know, what's making the news is somebody's knee is getting bashed. You know, not what's happening in educational reform in this country. Not how do we correct the welfare system. They show how bad it is, but they offer no solutions. They don't show the positive work that is being done in any sector of our society. They only focus on the negative, and that's what's rewarded with the story.

> *Author's Note: I take full responsibility for making an editorial decision to turn from journalism to something of more interest to me, and I would hope, of more concern to readers who possibly suspect that most journalists don't know the first thing about the world to come.*

DAVID:

Let's talk a little bit about eternity, what it means to you.

SARA:

I think the only way I can answer that is to say I don't know what eternity means. I think that the way I relate to whatever life force there is that sustains us all is to try to develop my inner core to be in harmony with it—whether we call it God or whatever we call it. I think I do call it God, and it means bringing into harmony all the forces of my life and finding that kind of peace so that I will be able to say when my time ends that I can return to the universe, that I can return to that great "whole" out there and be a worthy component of it.

I think there's an energy force out there. I don't think any of us is ever lost. I think we all return to that energy field or force, and I think at last we find peace. And I think the peace that we find in our own center is a reflection of what we will experience ultimately.

Ravy Bradford Dick, our 10-year-old daughter who had also spent the night with my wife, Lalie, and me at Fern Hill, brought in from the tree-mantled hillside alongside the small creek running down over rock patterns behind Sara's cabin a large handful of small, bell-shaped flowers in hues of lavender.

She handed them to Sara.

"Oh, Ravy! Judge used to pick these for me, and I haven't had anyone pick any of these for me for over two years," said Sara.

"What are they called?"

"Phlox, a wild phlox. Oh, they're going in a vase and they're going to stay on the kitchen table. Oh, they have to go in a vase right now. I'm going to get out a Waterford crystal vase that I never use. I save it for special moments. These are *wonderful*. I didn't think I'd ever get any of these picked for me again."

While Sara cooked Sunday breakfast—eggs, over easy, biscuits and gravy, sausage, and coffee—Lalie and I walked out onto the back porch, leaned on the railing, and looked up to what Jesse Stuart would have called the "Trees of Heaven."

"Tell me, talk with me, about the shortness of life and the value of understanding this reality," I said to Lalie, my soul mate, as we stood for a time there on the back porch of Sara's cabin on that morning in spring, when at first there were much crashing and booming of lightning and thunder, but then—a wonderful, softly and steadily falling rain.

"Oh, I don't know, sometimes I feel so small in the mix of things. We are all here for such a short period of time and when we go, for a certain time we are remembered, but little by little we become less and less a memory and more a part of the earth from whence we came. I have a hard time believing that this planet, our earth, is so small—smaller than the equivalent of one cell in the universe—and it astounds me to think about how tiny we are within that one cell. It is remarkable how many of us on this small place blow ourselves out of proportion by thinking we are grander than something that has lasted for billions of years. It saddens me to think that way.

"Sometimes I have a hard time holding onto my faith, my religious beliefs, especially in light of our small time-frame of existence. How could any or all of our religions mean anything, but then, who started all of this, and how? It really is rather a puzzlement. And you wonder why we came to be here on this earth and not on one of any of the other planets within the billions of galaxies out there."

"What does peace at the center mean to *you*?"

"You. You, you, and you. Without you I wouldn't have *my* peace at the center. Without you, I wouldn't have my life."

"But after I'm gone, there'll be you."

"But I will still have you. There is Ravy. We'll be the ones to do the remembering and that will be important to us. Right now, in this time I have, I just want to do the best I possibly can for the three of us because we are a small universe unto ourselves, and we are the ones who matter most to us. We really don't matter to anyone else—but God."

Our Peace At The Center

"Drop thy still dews of quietness, till all our strivings cease;
take from our souls the strain and stress,
and let our ordered lives confess
the beauty of thy peace."

– John Greenleaf Whittier –

"Preying will not be our object;
praying will be our peaceful pursuit."

– David Dick –

*T*he first coolness of late summer has arrived, the reward for patience during hot days and nights when the soil was packed tight by the sun's relentless rays.

"Could we have a little fire tonight?"

"Don't see why not."

The chimney sweep came early this year. The flues are clean and clear. There's a new damper in the bedroom fireplace chimney. Tonight will be the night for a small fire, a little brandy, and thee.

The only way, for me at least, to appreciate fully the sweetness of the annual event is to be here in the commonwealth throughout each of the seasons and the interseasons, too. The soft rhythms are best enjoyed when savored in sequence. It's only the beginning of more joys to come. A blue denim jacket felt good this morning, warm as a lifelong friendship. There was a thin glaze on the windshield of Old Blue, a reminder of colder mornings ahead. It's time for a little fencing project and some more sowing.

The fescue seed from Paris will be spread on the sides of the new farm road running up the steep hill, where we'll build our cabin in the sky, up where the winds cut across from the Rock Ridge Road. And when the cabin of our dreams is built, we'll have two big rocking chairs on the edge of creation. We'll have the same view of the hollows as the hawks, soaring as serenely as they, capturing the currents of the Indian summer nights and days.

For now, the big house in the valley will shelter us from the coming of fall and winter, and it will be good. The gathering of wood, postponed until now, will commence. It's the hugging time— the embracing of loved ones, full-circled, the scent of firewood cradled to the chin. It's the foot-patting time—the humming of tunes, the harmony of all we do and say as the days wind down to their too-precious few. The sheep are ready for their second shearing of the year. Chilled for a time, they'll appreciate a change of clothes when Indian summer warmth becomes "unseasonably" hot. The wool will hardly pay for the shearing, but it will be done more as a favor to the ewes, rams, and lambs than it will be for the sake of profits. Much of the "profit" on the farm is small change compared to the windfall of pleasure accompanying the slowing of summer and the phasing in of fall. The best is neither taxable nor bankable, and yet we are richly blessed. We have a quality of life that knows not boundary. Nature is profoundly democratic, treating everyone equally. Unfortunately, many of God's children rely upon the artificialities of a culture whose first love is conspicuous consumption.

Different marchers to different drummers draw deeply of new autumnal air, having nothing whatsoever to do with televised "entertainment." There's another way, a better way, and it's not too late in the year to enjoy it. Nothing is required except the willingness to stand still for a while to allow the silent beauty to wash over our faces and our hands.

What's the hurry? Where are we going? What are we going to do when we arrive there? How long will we stay? When will we be returning? Will the trip have mattered as much as we think?

I should want it to be said when anyone is asked 100 years from now, where were they and what were they doing, "They were upon the hill or down in the valley, and they were just standing or sitting there, not seeming to be going anywhere, yet their smiles bespoke expanding, peaceful thoughts. They weren't saying anything, at least not very much were they speaking, for their love had grown past the awkwardnesses of accumulated discourse. They weren't doing anything exactly at that moment, content in the drawing unto themselves of one of God's greatest gifts—cool, fresh air."

They seemed at peace with themselves and the world.

Afterword

By

Dr. Thomas D. Clark

Afterword

Historian Laureate for Life, Historian Emeritus of the
University of Kentucky, Eastern Kentucky University, and
Indiana University, Thomas D. Clark at age 91 continues to
write prolifically and with distinction from his home in
Lexington, Kentucky. He is eminently qualified to judge the
importance and lasting value of David Dick's writings from
Plum Lick, the setting for Peace at the Center. Dr. Clark
recognizes the continuation of the work of a promising new
voice for modern agrarianism in America.

*E*very thoughtful man or woman has at one time or another sought the true meaning and condition of peace—that is, peace to level out the ridges and valleys of life. There is no time in an individual's life when anticipation of peace of mind, of contentment with community, and most of all, with contemplation of place and past, comes into clearer focus than on the fortnight after retirement. So many questions have to be answered, and decisions within a new context have to be made.

In search of that center of peace, or of contentment and satisfaction, David Dick has brought before the bar of memory a multiplicity of experiences, of human conditions, and of lives spent according to the dictates of the times and events, which have drawn individuals into the vortex of contradictions and of choosing issues. He has reached back deep into the repository of time to find classical conformations of his values and judgments. At a more tangible level of time and near associations, he has called forth those plain but deeply essential people who made the earliest imprints on the land, and who raised monuments not of towering marble, but of the simple folkways in which the web of lives of generations has been woven to become the all-enmeshing web of folk mores.

The geography of David Dick's seating of centers of peace has often been as rugged as the physical geography of places. It stretches from the hearthstone of an ancestral home on the banks of Plum Lick Creek, crosses the ranges of news reporting for a major television network to the Alamo, to the plains of an Alabama upheaval caught in the furies of a storm of social change, to the halls of a university where classroom teachers struggle while the eternal tides of learning break against hardened administrative barriers.

David Dick presents against the unfolding canvas of time a tremendously intriguing view of the fiery center of the segregation storm, George Wallace. Unfolding on the pages of Dick's book is a view of a man whose political life was cut short by life-threatening bullets, but his moral, physical, and spiritual life was extended well into a period when he would recall, review, and revisit positions taken in the past. The saga of George Wallace is one of the complexities of the human condition cast in the mold of judicial mandate and sweeping institutional revisions of political and human values. The George Wallace whom David Dick saw on the campaign trail, and then as a badly wounded man, appears far more philosophical and humane than the one who threatened to stand in the schoolhouse doorway. George Wallace may well be a man who has searched for inner peace, and he may have found it in the acceptance of the inevitabilities of history itself.

The interview with Sara Combs almost has both the deep spiritual and philosophical qualities of a Grecian drama. In her conversation with David Dick she revealed both the mind and perceptive attitude toward the joys and tragedies of life of a modern Santayana or a

J. LARKINS

William Butler Yeats. Sara's penetrating portrayal of life with her complex husband, Bert Combs, is an incisive glimpse at a man who in his public mode wielded enormous personal influence; yet as the master of Fern Hill, tucked away in the Powell County hills, he was once again a son of the land, finding peace in the simplicities of the soil.

No doubt, future historians and biographers will weigh over and over again the history of the Bert Combs era in Kentucky, the persona of the man himself, the after-governor years in which he helped to blaze a new path to the future in raising the standards of a deficient school system. Few Kentucky governors have rendered as much public service in their post-administrative years. Sara's insights will ever be a gauge by which the historians and biographers will measure their appraisals and interpretations.

David Dick has written a book that searches for the innermost promises of peace and dignity to human life, at whatever level the individual chooses to live it. With the heart and soul of a rural Kentucky Thomas Hardy, he gives meaning and dignity to the simple things that form the matrix of living as much as possible on one's own terms on the land, yet having to be a part of a way of life attuned to a radically different tempo. It would be hard to imagine a greater contrast than that of a university professor almost literally holding a briefcase in one hand and a foundling lamb in the other, or, maybe, dealing with individualistic farm dogs by night, and less-than-willing students by day. That's enough to turn one's thoughts to the real center of spiritual and emotional peace.

For those of us who spring from the land and its rich patina of folkways, our dreams of place in a former setting grow brighter with age. Too, for those of us who have passed through that narrow gate of retirement, which ends one way of life and opens the door on another, there is always present in mind the weighing and evaluating of the experiences and values in life itself. We all carry within our psyche a center of peace; whether it be fully satisfying or not, it is there embedded in our very souls. We all have a sense of loyalty to place to which we can retreat in our reveries, if not in physical form.

For all of us, David Dick in his search for the peaceful center has led us along many of the main roads of a professional life with graphic delineations. He has guided us along the great webwork of back-country trails that pass through scenes of life as it has been lived for generations. He has ferreted out those small events, human and animal associations, the passing of one generation and the rise of another. There perhaps is no stable center of peace that is complete peace. Like the foot of a brilliant rainbow the promise is always there, and we all pursue it in our own way. David Dick has with profound sensitivity and devotion prepared a recipe for pursuing the search.

Thomas D. Clark

ACKNOWLEDGEMENTS

"Gratitude is the heart's memory."

– French Proverb –

I am especially grateful to Sara Combs, the widow of Governor Bert T. Combs, for inviting me into her home at Fern Hill, into her mind and into her heart. She taught me much. She answered all my questions and shared with me all the details as she knew them to be of her lover's death on December 3, 1991. Sara caused me to read Antoine de Saint-Exupéry's *The Little Prince*, and for that alone I am in her considerable debt. "Pee Jib" or "Jibbo," as Judge Combs called her during the 13 years of their time together, stirred within me a far better understanding of "peace at the center," the comforting knowledge that while I am here in this form, this imprisoning shell for only a short time and in the farthest reaches of spiritual life, I will rejoice with all God's creatures in the stardust of eternity.

I am grateful to Governor George C. Wallace, who endured me as a reporter for three presidential campaigns and who in 1994 honored my request to visit with him at his bedside in Montgomery, Alabama. Few human beings have suffered as much for their beliefs.

I should like to thank my former wife, Rose, for her encouragement and for sharing with me the way her mother baked bread, how her father pressed grapes into wine, how he loved his garden so intensely, and how he and his young bride came from Sicily to help build America.

I owe continuing appreciation to Dr. Thomas D. Clark, Historian Laureate of the Commonwealth of Kentucky, for his abiding friendship, his willingness to read my manuscripts and to comment extensively on them, and especially his smile and soft Mississippi voice each time we meet out on the trail of books.

Special thanks are extended to one of the commonwealth's finest editors, Gary Luhr. *Kentucky*

225

Living magazine is the result of Gary's remarkable talents, and the back page of each monthly issue, which carries my "The View from Plum Lick," has become a major turning point in my life as a writer. It was Gary who pointed me in the direction of Claude L. Brock of Concord Publishers and Brock-Kalvar Associates in Louisville, who in turn has seen in this manuscript a message that should be heard nationally.

The work of Jackie Larkins, who has illustrated both *Peace At The Center* and *The View From Plum Lick*, is as splendid as it is appreciated. His is a kind and sensitive soul.

The University of Kentucky has suffered me kindly, and for each individual instance of help, I say my sincerest thanks, especially to the doctors, nurses, and staff at the Albert Benjamin Chandler Medical Center and the Lucille Parker Markey Cancer Center. Thanks, too, to the retirement fund managers at CBS News for helping me to pay my mounting medical bills.

My gratitude is extended again to Carole A. Boyd for meticulously going over the manuscript, ferreting out errors too numerous to count, recommending cuts that I lacked the good sense to make. Wherever other mistakes occur in this book of a "better truth," they are mine, all mine, and for each one I ask forgiveness.

My thanks also go to Dean Douglas A. Boyd, who endured me for seven years, and who brought his sense of humor to the hospital, made me laugh in spite of everything that was happening to my body, and caused me to want to get out of bed even quicker so I could park my pickup truck in the same lot as his Volvo.

These acknowledgements would be incomplete without recognition of Roy L. Moore, a native of the Eastern Kentucky mountains, who as acting director of the University of Kentucky School of Journalism and Telecommunications was a constant encouragement for me to keep writing. Roy is the "seed corn" the late Governor Bert T. Combs said we should not lose.

Peace at the Center is dedicated to Lalie, my own sure and shining "pee jib"— editor, typesetter, graphic designer, confidante, healer, totally unselfish soul mate—who understands that we stand on the edges of all our vulnerabilities, looking for strength, accepting it when it comes, loving it while it lasts, finally letting go when the time arrives, as it did for Judge, to "go out on high tide."

ABOUT THE AUTHOR

David Dick, author of *The View from Plum Lick* and *Follow the Storm*—shepherd, farmer, educator, retired CBS News correspondent— is a sixth-generation Kentuckian to live in a remote corner of a valley purchased with English Crowns by his ancestors 200 years ago.

Born in Cincinnati, Ohio, in 1930, David Dick was 18 months old when his father died. David's mother returned with her three small children to her native rural Kentucky, where David would begin his formal education. There were 12 students in his high school graduation class in the small community of North Middletown. He earned the Bachelor and Master of Arts degrees in English Literature from the University of Kentucky.

During the Korean Conflict, David Dick served four years as a communicator with the United States Navy. He joined CBS News in 1966. In 1972 he received an Emmy for his coverage of the shooting of Gov. George C. Wallace. He was the founding publisher of *The Bourbon Times*, a weekly newspaper, which during a period of two years under his leadership, won 117 awards for excellence.

In 1985, following his retirement after 19 years at CBS, David Dick joined the faculty of his alma mater, and for six years was director of the UK School of Journalism. In 1987, he was inducted into the Kentucky Journalism Hall of Fame. After 10 years as a teacher of writing and journalism, David Dick plans to retire again to devote the rest of his life to writing. He is presently working on an historical novel, *Cynthia*.

David Dick is married to the former Eulalie "Lalie" Cumbo of New Orleans, Louisiana, and Woodville, Mississippi. They have one daughter, Ravy Bradford Dick. David is also the father of four adult children—Sam, Deborah, Catherine, and Nell—by a previous marriage.

227